What the experts are

101 Things Everyone Should

"*101 Things Everyone Should Know About Math* truly illustrates the scope and importance of learning and understanding mathematics. It is a fabulous resource for kids, parents and teachers looking for a way to link mathematics to everyday life. With entertaining connections to popular culture, sports, hobbies, science and careers, kids of all ages will find this book engaging...and challenging!"

—Carole Basile, Ed.D., University of Colorado, Denver, and Co-Director, Rocky Mountain Middle School Math and Science Partnership

"*101 Things Everyone Should Know About Math!* is great for practice and exploration. The puzzles and activities are entertaining and smartly connected to real life. Whether you are an expert or a novice, you'll find the challenges to be intriguing and insightful!"

—Maria Diamantis, Ed.D., Professor of Mathematics Education, Southern Connecticut State University

"*101 Things Everyone Should Know About Math* is an extraordinary resource—imaginative and practical, insightful and humorous. Students will not only have fun solving the problems, but they will also find it an invaluable aid with homework. As a former high school math teacher, I love that this book carries mathematics out of the world of the elite and translates it into a language we can all understand."

—Alvin Mayes, BA Mathematics, Department of Dance (and Math tutor), University of Maryland

"A wonderful collection of facts and trivia that can inspire children of all ages to think about and use math in their lives. The breadth of coverage and easy-to-understand explanations inside this little book can make math a subject of interest and relevance for all."

—Patrick Farenga, co-author of *Teach Your Own: The John Holt Book of Homeschooling*

"This book is a wonderful secondary resource for all teachers of mathematics. Students need the real-world math skills that the activities in this book reinforce. The challenges are enjoyable, yet they require higher-level thinking—children barely realize they are actively learning! *101 Things Everyone Should Know About Math* is an invaluable tool for students, teachers and parents!"

—Dr. Cheryl Moretz, Principal, Brayton Elementary School, Summit, NJ

DISCOVER WHY EVERYONE LOVES *101 Things Everyone Should Know About Science*

Awarded the highly regarded "**NSTA Recommends**" by the National Science Teachers Association, the world's largest organization promoting excellence in science teaching.

NAPPA Honors Winner
National Parenting Publications operates the most comprehensive awards program for Children's Products and Parenting Resources.

Endorsed by **Science Magazine**: "This book could be called 'How to Learn Science Without Really Trying!'... provides answers in a succinct, cleverly written, and understandable format... should be on everyone's bookshelf!"

Endorsed by the **Carnegie Academy for Science Education**: "...provides clear and engaging explanations of complex phenomena... encourages a lifetime of curiosity about the world around us!"

WonderQuest

Endorsed by **WonderQuest, the Globe and Mail's on-line Science Column**: "...challenges, intrigues us, and leads us on a voyage of discovery....captures science with pithy and engaging explanations!"

Midwest Book Review: ★★★★ "...a compendium of diverse fun science facts suitable for inquiring minds from 8 to 80!"

Dia L. Michels and Nathan Levy
ISBN: 978-0-9678020-5-3
Paperback, Ages 8 to 12
160 pages, 8.5" x 5.5"
$9.95

Teaching the science of everyday life

101 Things Everyone Should Know About Math

By Marc Zev, Kevin B. Segal and Nathan Levy

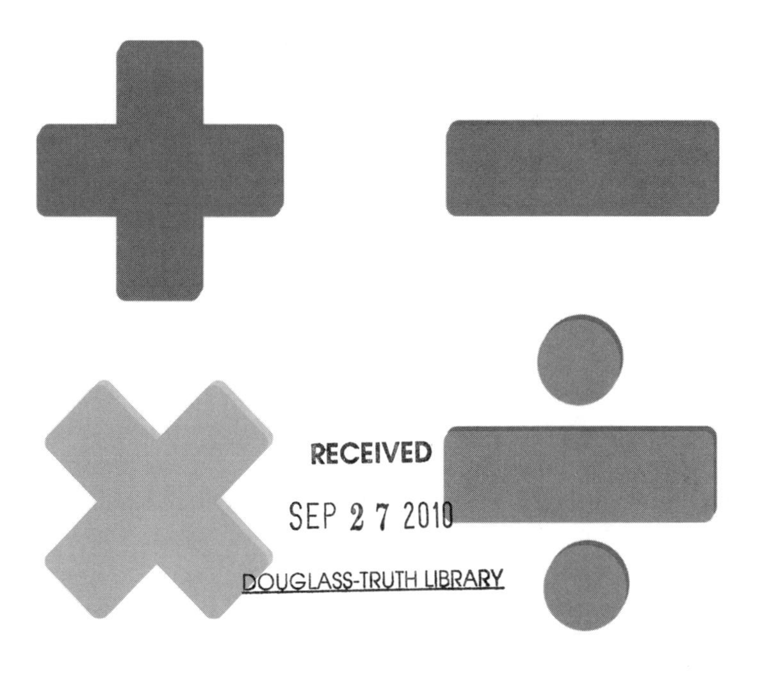

Science, Naturally!, LLC
Washington, DC

1st edition • April 2010 • ISBN: 0-9678020-3-2 / ISBN 13: 978-0-9678020-3-9

Ebook edition • April 2010 • ISBN: 0-9700106-3-X / ISBN 13: 978-0-9700106-3-6

Published in the United States by
Science, Naturally!
725 8th Street, SE
Washington, DC 20003
(202) 465-4798 / Toll-free: 1-866-SCI-9876 (1-866-724-9876)
Fax: (202) 558-2132
Info@ScienceNaturally.com / www.ScienceNaturally.com

Distributed to the book trade in the United States by
National Book Network
(301) 459-3366 / Toll-free: 1-800-787-6859 / Fax: (301) 429-5746
CustServ@nbnbooks.com / www.nbnbooks.com

Cover, Book Design and Section Illustrations by Andrew Barthelmes, Peekskill, NY

Library of Congress Cataloging-in-Publication Data

Zev, Marc, 1961-
101 things everyone should know about math / Marc Zev, Kevin B. Segal and Nathan Levy. -- 1st ed.
p. cm.
Includes bibliographical references and index.
ISBN 978-0-9678020-3-9
1. Mathematics--Popular works. 2. Mathematics--Juvenile literature. I.
Segal, Kevin B., 1964- II. Levy, Nathan, 1945- III. Title. IV. Title: One hundred one things everyone should know about math. V. Title: One hundred and one things everyone should know about math.
QA93.Z48 2009
510--dc22
2008049633

10 9 8 7 6 5 4 3 2 1

Schools, libraries, government and non-profit organizations can receive a bulk discount for quantity orders. Please contact us at the address above or email us at Info@ScienceNaturally.com.
Test booklets available (ISBN: 978-0-9678020-2-2). Please contact us at the address above.

Printed in the United States of America

Dedication

To Jackie, Jonathan and Benjamin, who keep me on my toes, challenge me at every turn, and, above all, keep me humble.
–Marc Zev

To Rachel, Abby and Daniel, who taught me the capacity for love is infinite. Also, thanks to everyone who understands that generating random numbers is too important to be left to chance.
–Kevin B. Segal

To my granddaughters, Sadie MacGuire and Taryn Koslow, two delightful young ladies (in Sadie's case, very young) who will influence society in positive ways. I love you both.
–Nathan Levy

Table of Contents

Introduction: Three Paths, One Target

Several years ago I founded a non-profit organization with the mission of teaching kids to be better problem solvers. As I met with various community leaders and educators, to introduce the Foundation for Innovative Learning to them, I spent a great deal of time in conversations where I would say "...problem solving...", and they would say things like "So, you teach math?" I would then have to explain again that "No, not math specifically, but strategies to make solving all problems easier." So, now after years of telling people that I don't teach math, here I am writing a book that teaches math.

Irony—you've got to love it!

Although my academic career was oriented towards engineering, it does make sense that I wound up writing a math book. Engineering, after all, is applied physics, and physics is applied math. The way I see it is: engineering is like a building, its structural framework is physics, and the tools used to construct the frame are math. You can't build the frame without the tools, and your building won't stand without the frame. Taking that analogy one step further: some people design tools, some design and build frames, and some people, myself included, take advantage of the other two groups to construct the buildings.

When you think of it that way, it is easy to see that the tools (the numbers and equations that make up math) are the key to everything. Although you use the tools to construct buildings, that is not their exclusive use. Math tools can also be used to build pretty much everything, from the Stock Market to farmers' fields, and from cosmetics to cars and planes. That is why it is so important to understand how to use math. No matter what career path you choose, math will be involved—even if it is just used to make sure your paycheck is correct.

101 Things Everyone Should Know About Math is not a math quiz book—it's a question and answer book that is designed to be a fun, light read that provides you with an understanding of when and how the real world uses math. I hope that it takes the "problem" out of problem solving and shows you that math is just like solving a puzzle—your answer depends upon the strategies you use to solve it.

In school, you learn the techniques of algebra by looking at problems and completing them using multiple methods. This book, on the other hand, is meant to show you that Algebra and Geometry are sneaky beasts and live in a lot of places that you might not expect. We will point out some of those places and tease out the math. Once you are introduced to these concepts and their common patterns, you'll recognize them in more and more places, and problems you had no idea how to solve in the past will become easier. This book will help you know which tools you should use to build a solution.

When you know how to use the tools, you can make anything. We can reverse the trend of demonizing math and those who are good at it. By dismissing math to the mathematicians, generations of people can't do basic computations and must rely on others and/or technology to do their math. Do we really want to be forced to trust every sales person because we don't understand how interest is calculated?

After writing this book, I volunteered to give a "guest lecture" in my son's fourth grade class. I brought in some appropriate problems from the book. I then walked the students through our way of doing the problems. I enjoyed the hour I spent at school, and the kids seemed to enjoy themselves, too. Afterwards, I received a stack of thank you letters from the kids. While they were all appropriately praising, a couple of the letters really stood out. One girl wrote, "I don't really like math, but you made it seem fun," which meant that I met one of my goals. A boy wrote, "I learned that math can and is a lot easear [sic] when you put your mind to it." Another small victory. This last letter left me with mixed feelings. A girl told me that I showed her the "fun side of math," which was gratifying. On the other hand, at the bottom of the page, she wrote: "12 x 12 = 264." I'm not really sure what to make of that. The fact that she voluntarily did math is a good thing, but the fact that her answer is incorrect helps me to see the need for more ways to teach basic math concepts in a memorable way that will inspire learners of all ages.

My hope is that you will realize that math is not something that should make you fearful or nervous. Instead, it is a tool—like a screwdriver, a tape measure, or a sphygmomanometer (the thing that goes on your arm to measure your blood pressure)—that can be used to make our lives better.

I wrote this book because I want people to be better problem solvers. Knowing how to use math is one step in achieving that goal. I also wrote this book for my children. Both my boys have taken pride in helping me work out some of the problems, and any project that makes your children proud is a good one.

My name is Kevin, and I love math. Growing up, I couldn't get enough of it. I kept my own baseball standings, calculated each team's winning percentage and determined my team's "magic number," even if it was 10 games into the season. I read freeway signs and would sum the distances to each street just to see if the fractions would add to a whole number.

To me, math is much more than a collection of facts, however interesting. Nor is math about who can do the most rapid calculations. What fascinates me about math is that while it is based on absolutely rigid principles, its application lends itself to creativity and intuition. It is as much art as it is science.

When I was a student, the teachers were always saying, "Show your work." The answer was not as important as the process of reaching the answer. Guessing was forbidden. Showing the process was the only way to demonstrate you understood the concepts. Creativity through alternate solutions was frowned upon.

In the business world, the situation is reversed. The answer is of primary importance. While creativity in achieving the answer is valued, determining the correct answer as quickly as possible is crucial. You will need to produce the process for reaching the answer only when necessary. You must find the answer yourself, because there is no answer at the back of the book (wouldn't it be nice if there was a book?).

My journey to the executive benefits industry was a rather indirect one. I entered college, as most students do, unprepared for the real world. Since I had enjoyed math in school, I became a math major until I could figure out something that I liked better. Ten years, two math degrees, and four years of doctoral work later, I still had found nothing I liked better than math. I also had six years of teaching undergraduates a variety of introductory math courses, which convinced me of two things. One was that teaching problem-solving strategies not found in the standard textbooks was interesting and challenging. The other was that it takes a special kind of person to have a full-time teaching career, and that wasn't going to be me.

Finally, I decided to become an actuary. Actuaries deal with the financial impact of risk and uncertainty. They help companies to calculate risk and to formulate policies that minimize the cost of that risk. It is also a way for someone deeply rooted in the study of mathematics to branch out into other areas of practice, including business, law, accounting and consulting. Unfortunately, the rumor that being an actuary is a boring job persists. I try to show people of all ages that the work I do is actually exciting and engaging—it just takes a little creativity.

At my firm, growth involves change. A decade ago, I was a "charismatic number cruncher." Today, I help train employees. Said another way, I'm back to being a teacher. The circle is complete.

How we share the excitement of math and science is constantly evolving.

Before, we were only interested in asking the right questions, and leaving our children to forage for answers themselves in the often daunting woods of mathematics. But recently, in my collaboration with Dia Michels on *101 Things Everyone Should Know About Science*, she and I created a book that not only asks questions, but also answers them along with the reader. Furthermore, the history and context of the lesson is explored, answering the eternal query of students everywhere, "Why do we need to know this?" (Believe me, after 35 years of being a teacher and principal, I've heard this plenty of times). *101 Things Everyone Should Know About Science* has also provided a valuable service to educators and parents.

In this new book, Marc Zev, Kevin Segal and I have created a problem-solving book that will challenge higher-level learners as well as provide educators and parents with basic math knowledge. It will furnish the blank walls of theory with colorful real-life analogies and examples, allow students to look at math through the lens of practical application, and transform math from an obligatory torture to a necessary tool.

101 Things Everyone Should Know about Math emphasizes critical and creative thinking by focusing on the math concepts that need more attention, or perhaps just a little more decoration. It will be a great supplement to share with my many workshop participants as I continue to speak around the United States and the world. It will provide a superior bridge from my current publications, *Creativity Day by Day, Thinking and Writing Activities for the Brain*, and *Nathan Levy's Stories With Holes*. I am proud to help bring this book to the world.

"I THINK YOU SHOULD BE
MORE EXPLICIT HERE IN STEP TWO."

How To Use This Book

This book is designed to be fun.

You can answer most of the questions in just a few minutes. Even though you can find most of the answers with mental math, you might like to have paper and pencil on hand. Writing down your ideas might help you think. You can answer the questions in any order, but it might be helpful to begin with the questions in the first chapter, "Facts, Just Math Facts," as a warm-up. The information in them will be useful later, and it will refresh your math skills.

Many people have trouble with math because it was not clearly explained to them how the equations can be used in real life. In this book, we will give examples of situations where understanding math concepts will help you solve everyday problems. You'll even learn techniques that can help you solve problems faster.

Read each question carefully, organize your thoughts and take your best shot. When you review the answers, take your time to understand the solutions to the problems and how to solve them. Once you understand that, we hope you will see the connection between the questions and the answers and how you can use them in your life. If you do that, you're doing a great job.

Above all—Have Fun!

Facts, Just Math Facts Questions

F+A+C+T+S=

Answer the questions in the following sections as best you can, then check your answers in the corresponding answer section. The answers to the math facts questions can be found starting on page 58.

1. Easy as Pi

On March 14th, Albert's school celebrated Pi Day. They had several pi-related events, including a pie sale. What was the price of each pie?

A. $1.43 C. $3.14
B. $2.31 D. $4.44

2. Hip To Be Squared

What is the square of 15?

HINT: The square of a number is that number multiplied by itself. Its notation is a superscripted '2'; a number x squared is written as x^2. For example, the square of 3 is written as 3^2 ($3 \times 3 = 9$). The square of 14 (14×14) is 196, and the square of 16 (16×16) is 256.

3. A Prime Number

Ogg, the caveperson, went hunting but didn't bring anything home. So, Nahtogg sent him to the butcher to buy some prime rib. Ogg returned with 4 bags of rib bones, each one containing a different quantity:

Bag A: 2 ribs Bag C: 4 ribs
Bag B: 3 ribs Bag D: 5 ribs

Nahtogg complained, "I send you to store for prime rib. One bag not prime rib, but composite rib. Go back to store and get all prime rib!"

Which bag made Nahtogg cranky?

NEED A CLUE? A prime number (also called a prime) is a whole number that has exactly 2 whole numbers (called "factors") that divide into it. The two factors are 1 and the prime number itself.

4. Following Orders

Solve the following: $7 \times 3 + 2 \div 4 - 2^2 \times (6 - 1)^2$

NEED A CLUE? The key to this problem is understanding which calculations you need to do first, a technique called "order of operations." In arithmetic and algebra, problems like the one above are evaluated using a universal set of operations.

These precedence rules are used in many computer programming languages and modern calculators. However, they are only tools that help you arrive at the answer and are not math "facts."

5. Given the Choice

What is the result when you multiply 107 by 23?

A. 1,811 C. 2,461
B. 1,986 D. 2,593

NEED A CLUE? Usually, when multiple answers are provided (as in this case), you can rule out one or two of the answers very simply. One of the easiest ways is to figure out whether the answer should be odd or even. If the numbers are both odd, then the answer will be odd. Otherwise, the answer will be even.

6. You Know the Drill

Joe has a $^3/_8$" wire that he needs to thread through a hole in a piece of wood. He wants the hole to be as small as possible, but still allow the wire to easily go through. His drill bits are all in metric units (millimeters). Which is the best drill bit to use?

A. 5 mm
B. 10 mm
C. 15 mm
D. 20 mm

7. Find it Fast

What is the product of 25 x 19?

8. Facts and Figures

Match up each geometric figure on the left with its correct name on the right.

A. 	1. Acute angle
B. 	2. Line segment
C. 	3. Right angle
D. 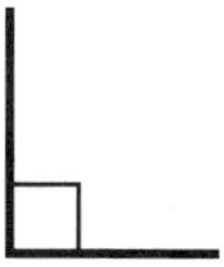	4. Ray
E. 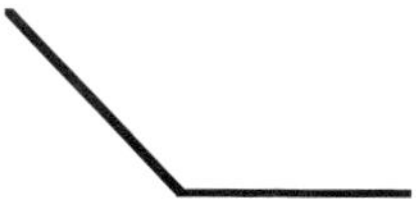	5. Obtuse angle
F. 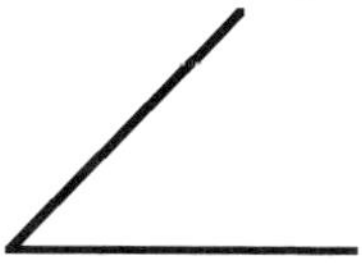	6. Line

9. Name That Polygon

A polygon (from Greek, meaning "many-angle") is a set of line segments, in the same plane, that connect end to end. The straight line segments that make up the polygon are called its sides or edges and the points where the sides meet are the polygon's vertices, or corners.

Here are the names of polygons with varying number of sides, from 3 sides to 10 sides. Put the names of the polygons in order from fewest sides to most sides.

A. Decagon
B. Octagon
C. Triagon (Triangle)
D. Pentagon
E. Heptagon
F. Nonagon
G. Hexagon
H. Tetragon (Quadrilateral)

10. Polygon Area

Put these regular geometric shapes in order of least to greatest area.

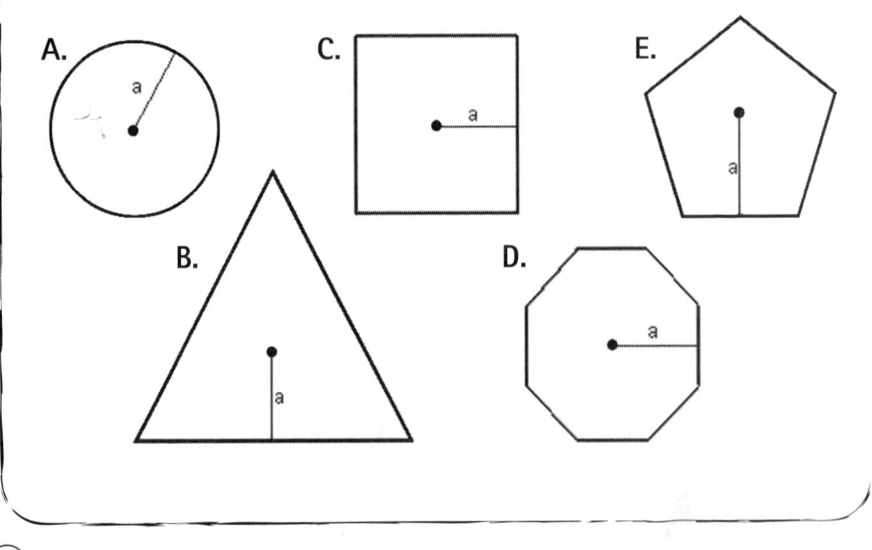

11. Polygon Area, the Sequel

Put these regular geometric shapes in order of least to greatest area.

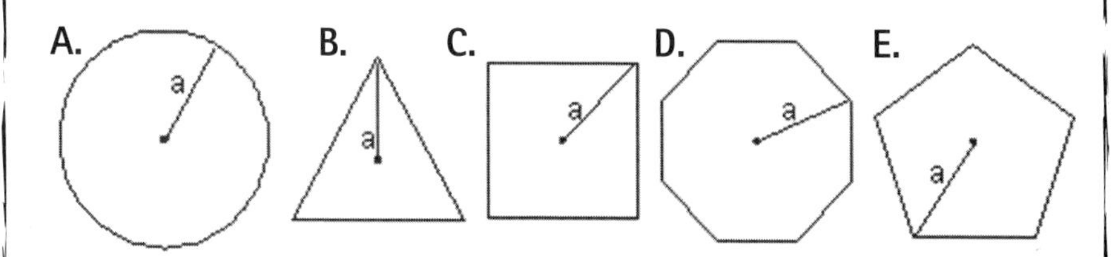

12. Show Me a Postcard

My 9th grade algebra teacher, Mr. Hronas, has a special picture frame that measures 3 feet by 2 feet. In it are postcards that students sent him from their vacations around the country. Each postcard is 4 inches tall by 6 inches wide, and none overlap. He can hang the frame either horizontally or vertically. What is the maximum number of postcards he can put in the frame?

13. The Great Pumpkins

As part of a science experiment, Habib is growing two pumpkins, each with its own special soil mixture. Every day, Habib weighs each pumpkin and measures its diameter. He needs to plot the data on a graph. Which of the graphs below should he use?

A.

B.

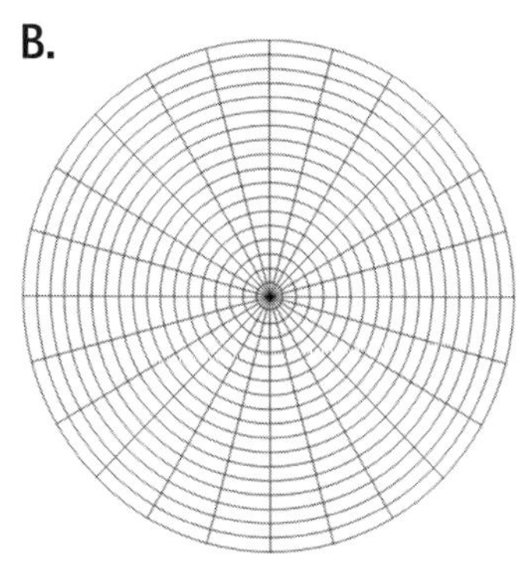

C.

D.

14. Over the Moon

Spencer, the space cadet, is flying 1,000 meters over an airless moon at a speed of 30 kilometers per hour (kph). He drops a marker to remind him to visit that area again. From the viewpoint of someone standing on the moon, which of the following trajectories (paths) is the marker most likely to take on its way down to the surface?

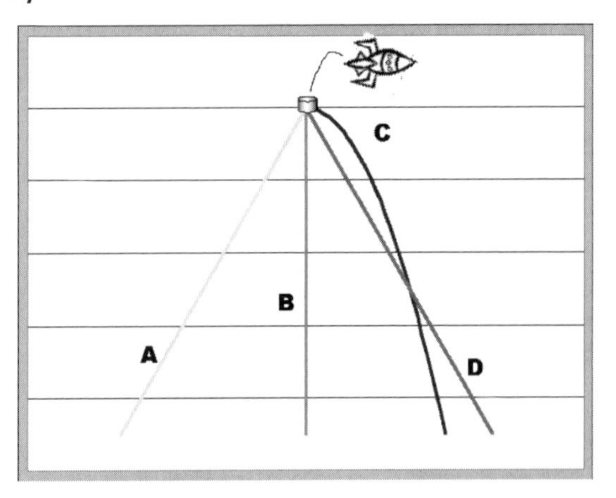

15. Father of Algebra

Who is considered the father of algebra?

A. Muhammad ibn Musa al-Khwarizmi
B. Euclid of Alexandria
C. Gottfried Wilhelm Leibniz
D. Leonhard Euler

NEED A CLUE? The source of the world "algebra" is an Arabic word: al-jabr.

16. Proof Positive

True or false: the following proves that 1=2:

Suppose $a = b$	
Multiply both sides by b	$ab = b^2$
Subtract a^2 from both sides	$ab - a^2 = b^2 - a^2$
Factor both sides	$a(b - a) = (b + a)(b - a)$
Cancel $(b - a)$ from both sides	$a = b + a$
Substitute a for b, since $a = b$	$a = a + a$ or $a = 2a$
Divide both sides by a	$1 = 2$

Health, Food & Nutrition

(The answers to these questions begin on page 73)

17. Pi and Pie

Since Albert loves pie, he planned on trying many kinds of different pies at his school's Pi Day celebration. The only problem is that Albert's mother told him he could eat no more than the equivalent of a quarter of a pie. Albert had enough money to purchase as many slices as he wanted. However, he had difficulty making his choices because not all the pies were cut into the same number of slices.

Type of Pie	Number of Slices per Pie
Strawberry	6
Apple	8
Cherry	10
Chocolate Cream	10
Banana Cream	12
Lemon Meringue	12
Boston Cream	16
Coconut Cream	16

What is the maximum number of slices of different pies Albert can buy so that he ends up with no more than the equivalent of $^1/_4$ of a pie?

NEED A CLUE? Start by choosing the pies that have the most slices per pie. These slices will be the smallest.

18. Smart Cookie

Inara is having a party and is going to make her famous Alphabet Cookies. To make sure everyone will get a cookie, she will make one and a half batches. Everything is going well until the recipe calls for $^1/_3$ cup of butter. Inara only has measuring cups in the following denominations: $^1/_8$ cup, $^1/_4$ cup, $^1/_3$ cup, $^1/_2$ cup & 1 cup.

Can Inara measure out the correct amount of butter using her measuring cups?

19. Half-Baked

Inara is having another party and is going to make her famous Alphabet Cookies again, but this time she wants to make only half a batch. Everything is going well until, yet again, the recipe calls for $^1/_3$ cup of butter. Inara still has only measuring cups in the following denominations: $^1/_8$ cup, $^1/_4$ cup, $^1/_3$ cup, $^1/_2$ cup & 1 cup.

Can Inara measure out the correct amount of butter using her measuring cups?

20. Tin Pan Tally

A cake recipe says to put batter into two 8" round pans, but you don't have any. Of the following, which combination of pans will work best?

A. Two 8" square pans
B. One 9" square pan
C. One 9" x 13" rectangular pan
D. Three 8" x 4" rectangular pans

21. Marshmallow Treats

A recipe calls for 5 cups (about 72 cubic inches) of large marshmallows. Unfortunately, you only have mini marshmallows. All the marshmallows are perfect cylinders. The large ones have a *diameter* of 1-inch and are 1-inch in height. The mini marshmallows are $^1/_2$ inch in *diameter* and $^1/_2$ inch in height. If you measure out 5 cups of mini marshmallows into a rectangular pan measuring 8" x 9" x 1" and you don't squish the marshmallows in, are you most likely to have:

A. A larger volume of marshmallows
B. A smaller volume of marshmallows
C. The same volume of marshmallows

22. Putting on the Zits

Jordan is a teenager. Therefore, there is a 25% chance he will wake up each morning with at least one pimple. For Jordan, it takes two days for each pimple to go away. If Jordan has no pimples on Thursday, what are the chances that Jordan will have at least one pimple by Saturday night?

A. 0% C. 88%
B. 44% D. 100%

NEED A CLUE? This one looks hard, but it is easier to figure out how likely it is for Jordan not to have any pimples. Here is the key: The exact opposite of having at least one pimple is not having any pimples.

23. Cricket Calories

While filming a reality TV show on a remote tropical island, you find yourself lacking enough calories to compete in the challenges. In the hope of surviving, you decide you must find something to eat, even if it isn't exactly to your usual tastes. There are plenty of insects on the island. Maybe you'd like to get the calories you need by munching on crickets.
How many calories are in 100 grams of crickets?

A. 1,727 calories
B. 121.5 calories
C. 179.5 calories

Nutritional Value of Various Insects per 100 grams

Insect	Protein (g)	Fat (g)	Carbohydrate(g)
Giant Water Beetle	19.8	8.3	2.1
Red Ant	13.9	3.5	2.9
Silk Worm Pupae	9.6	5.6	2.3
Dung Beetle	17.2	4.3	0.2
Cricket	12.9	5.5	5.1
Large Grasshopper	20.6	6.1	3.9
Small Grasshopper	14.3	3.3	2.2
June Beetle	13.4	1.4	2.9
Caterpillar	6.7	N/A	N/A
Termite	14.2	N/A	N/A
Weevil	6.7	N/A	N/A

Data collected from The Food Insects Newsletter, July 1996 (Vol. 9, No. 2, ed. by Florence V. Dunkel, Montana State University) and Bugs In the System, by May Berenbaum

NEED A CLUE? Here's how to calculate how many calories you can get from insects: Calories = 4 x (carbohydrate + protein) + 9 x (fat), where carbohydrates, protein and fat are measured in grams.

24. Going Buggy

As you explore the island, you find there are alternatives to the crickets. You discover a large colony of red ants, a colony of termites and an endless supply of June beetles. Use the nutritional chart in question 23 to decide which will provide you with the most calories.

A. Red ants
B. Termites
C. June beetles

NEED A CLUE? You can figure this out without any calculations. Look at the formula: Calories = 4 x (carbohydrate + protein) + 9 x (fat). Note that the amount of fat is the most important factor.

25. Pizza Combo

You've got 22 hungry football players back at the house, and you're out looking for pizza. Each player wants his own pizza, which consists of one kind of crust, one kind of cheese, and one topping. They don't care what they get as long as nobody gets the same pizza. You have three pizza parlors to choose from:

- Mama Cass – they've got 1 kind of crust, 1 kind of cheese and 18 different toppings
- Tiddly's – 2 kinds of crust, 2 kinds of cheese and 5 different toppings
- Shack o' Pizza – 3 kinds of crust, 3 kinds of cheese and 3 different toppings.

From which pizza place are you going to order the pizza?

A. Mama Cass
B. Tiddly's
C. Shack o' Pizza
D. You're out of luck; none of the places can make what you need. You get to spend another year as the tackling dummy.

26. Pizza Combo Part 2

Apparently, one pizza wasn't enough. You are now being sent to the pizza parlor that can give you the greatest number of two topping pizzas (Each pizza must have two different toppings on it). Where are you going?

A. Mama Cass
B. Tiddly's
C. Shack o' Pizza
D. To another school that doesn't have such hungry football players

27. Dough Boy

Wolfgang is making bread. After he mixes the flour, water, yeast and all the other ingredients together, he has a four-cup glob of dough. He then puts the dough in a bowl, covers it, and puts it in a warm place to rise. After the dough doubles in volume, Wolfgang punches down the dough so it loses $^1/_3$ of its volume. He then allows the dough to double in size again, before he puts it in the oven to bake.

How big a bowl does he need so that the dough does not pop over the top or ooze over the sides?

A. 1 quart C. $^1/_2$ gallon
B. 6 pints C. 75 oz

NEED A CLUE? Begin by figuring how many cups of dough there are after all the rising and punching and rising again. Then convert the cups to another kind of measurement.

28. Sugar and Spice

Farmer Kabibble is famous for his hot chocolate. When he makes a cup for himself he uses 1 $^1/_3$ tablespoons of unsweetened cocoa powder; 3 tablespoons of sugar; $^1/_2$ teaspoon of the Farmer's special spices; and 1 cup of a super secret blend of milk, cream, vanilla and boiling water.
The local high school has asked Farmer Kabibble to make a 100-cup vat of his hot chocolate so they can sell it as a fundraiser at their football game.

How much cocoa powder will Farmer Kabibble need to make 100 cups of his famous hot chocolate?

A. $3^1/_2$ cups C. $8^1/_3$ cups
B. $5^3/_4$ cups D. 10 cups

29. Hard Pill to Swallow

Each morning Xander must take a pill containing 100 mg of medicine. Let's assume that the medicine is immediately introduced into his system. Among other things, our bodies work to wash foreign stuff out, including medicine. Because of this process, in 24 hours, Xander's body will wash out 40% of the existing amount of medicine in his body. Xander takes his medicine at 8:00 a.m. each morning. If he takes it for the first time on Monday, how much medicine is in his body just before he takes his dose on Wednesday?

A. 64 mg C. 128 mg
B. 96 mg

30. Worth the Weight

The body mass index (BMI) is a formula designed to identify the relative weight range of a person based on the person's height. The accepted range for good health is 18.5 to 25. The formula for body mass index is:

$$\text{BMI} = \frac{\text{weight (kg)}}{\text{height x height (m x m)}}$$

It was formulated in metric units (kg/m^2). However, in the United States, we typically use pounds to measure weight and inches to measure height. If we use these units to measure BMI instead of the metric units, then the BMI tables have to be altered. Will using pounds and inches cause the best BMI range numbers for good health to be higher or lower?

Travel Questions

(The answers for these questions can be found on page 86.)

31. Dim Bulb Racing

Dim Bulb Racing Promoters Inc. has organized an airplane race around the world. To make sure the pilots don't get in each other's way, they have planned for each plane to start on the same longitude line, but on different latitude lines. The pilots must stay on their own latitude lines throughout the race. You will fly in the race. By random drawing you are the first to choose the latitude line on which you will fly. Which of the following latitudes will you pick?

A. 45°S　　C. 30°N

B. 0°　　D. 60°N

NEED A CLUE? Remember that latitude lines run east to west, parallel to the Equator (latitude 0°). All longitude lines run between the North and South poles. They all intersect each other at the two poles. The line of longitude that is designated at 0° is called the Prime Meridian. An easy way to remember the difference is to think of latitude lines as rungs on a ladder. Think of longitude lines as long.

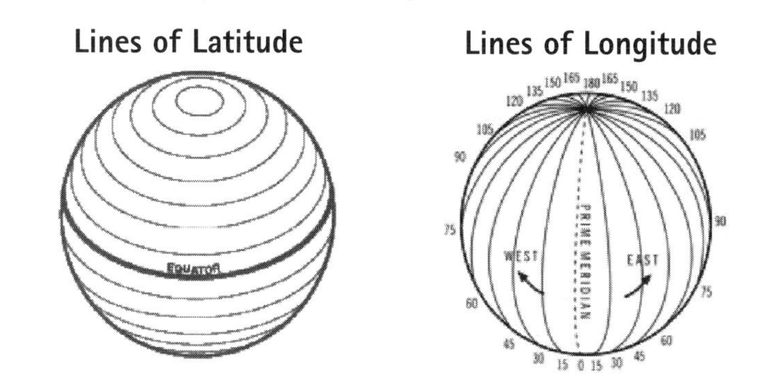

32. Zoning Out

The continental United States has four time zones: the Pacific, Mountain, Central and Eastern Time Zones. There are 24 time zones around the world. If you were to estimate how many degrees of longitude enclose the continental US based on time zones, how many degrees would there be from California to Maine?

A. 5° to 25°   C. 60° to 90°
B. 30° to 60°

NEED A CLUE? There are 360° in a circle and 24 time zones defined for the earth. So, ideally, each time zone is made up of $360° \div 24 = 15°$ of longitude.

33. Instantaneous Travel

Louise flies on a commercial airline from Louisville, Kentucky, to St. Louis, Missouri. As the plane takes off, she notices the time is 1:00 p.m. She has time for just a couple of Sudoku puzzles before the plane lands and the flight attendant announces, "Welcome to St. Louis, where the time is 1:00 p.m." Louise is convinced the flight attendant can't tell time, but sure enough, it is 1:00 p.m. in St. Louis. What happened?

34. Flying to Florida

Glen wants to fly from Los Angeles, California to Orlando, Florida to watch baseball spring training. His airline ticket looks like this:

From			To	
3/11	LAX	11:00 a.m.	ORL	7:00 p.m.
3/18	ORL	11:00 a.m.	LAX	1:00 p.m.

Glen notices that it takes 8 hours to fly from California to Florida, but only takes 2 hours to fly back. What's going on?

35. Ticket to Ride

Maya rides the train to work every weekday and rarely takes a day off. During normal months, she can spend either $25 for 1 round-trip ticket, $70 for a pack of 5 round-trip tickets, or $240 for a monthly pass. In December, the rail line offers a 25% discount on the monthly pass. After working all year, Maya finally wants to take some time off in December. As it turns out, she will only be working 8 days that month. What combination of passes/tickets should she buy?

36. There and Back Again

Zach lives a mile from school. It takes him 15 minutes to ride his bike to school, but only 5 minutes to ride home (There's a lesson on motivation here, but that's beside the point). What is Zach's average speed?

A. 4 miles per hour C. 8 miles per hour
B. 6 miles per hour D. 12 miles per hour

37. Get Me to School on Time!

You are riding your bike to school, which is 10 miles from your house. You know that you have to average 10 miles per hour to get to school on time. When you are half way there you realize you have averaged only 5 mph. How fast do you have to go on the remaining half of the trip to get to school on time?

A. 15 mph C. 30 mph
B. 20 mph D. You can't possibly get there on time

38. Going the Extra Mileage

Jackie drives a new hybrid car that keeps track of the gas usage as miles per gallon (mpg). Jackie knows that the rate of gas consumption varies based on how fast she accelerates and whether she is going up or downhill. Usually, Jackie averages 50 mpg.

On one trip from her house to the beach 50 miles away, Jackie notices that she has only managed 40 mpg. Jackie decides she wants her average back up to 50 mpg. So, on the way home, following the same path, Jackie works to average 60 mpg, and does. However, when she arrives home she finds that her average gas usage for the whole day is not 50 mpg, but 48 mpg. Why?

39. Sprockets

Bob has a new mountain bike with three sprockets in the front and six sprockets in the back. Each sprocket, front and back, is a different size. Bob can use each possible combination of sprockets to make a "gear." Each gear gives him an advantage in speed or in riding up and down hills. How man different "gears" does the bike have?

40. Moon Landing

The country of Grand Fenwick wants to explore several locations along the equator of the moon. They hire Dim Bulb Aerospace to build a rocket powerful enough to get to the moon. After the moon-lander touches down, the astronauts will explore the area and then move 100 miles along the equator to a new location.

Dim Bulb tells the Grand Fenwick Space Agency that to save money and complications, the moon-lander can't move sideways—just up and down. When the astronauts want to change locations, they must take off in the lander, hover above the surface as the moon rotates below, and finally land in a new location.

According to Dim Bulb's estimates, the circumference of the moon at the equator is 5,600 miles and the period of the moon (how long it takes to spin completely around once on its axis) is 28 days. If Dim Bulb's theory and numbers are correct, how long will the astronauts have to be off the surface of the moon to land 100 miles from where they started?

NEED A CLUE? If the circumference of the moon is 5,600 miles, then 100 miles would be $^1/_{56}$ of the distance around the moon. If it takes 28 days for the moon to fully spin around its axis, in one day it would travel $^1/_{28}$ of the way around. So you can figure that $^1/_{56}$ the circumference is half of $^1/_{28}$ the circumference.

41. June Bugs

Stacey, Tracey, Macy and Clyde all play in a band called the June Bugs. They travel from one performance to the next in Tracey's van. The van gets 15 miles per gallon.

Their agent has lined up two possible gigs for them on Saturday night. One is at the City A Auditorium, pays $200 and is 15 miles away. The second possible gig is at the City B Bistro, pays $300 and is 150 miles away. Take into account that the agent will get 10% of the fee off the top (meaning they have to pay their agent first before expenses) and consider that gas costs $3 a gallon.

Which gig will be a better deal for the June Bugs?

42. Around the World

When Ferdinand Magellan set off to be the first to circumnavigate the world, he requested that each ship in his expedition carry 18 hourglasses.

Magellan's plan was for some of the hourglasses to run for 30 minutes, some to run for one hour, some to run for two hours and some to run for four hours. All of the hourglasses were the same size, but each had different amounts of sand to measure the time.

Imagine that the hourglasses were made by making two empty cones out of glass and connecting them point to point. In order for the sand to flow correctly, the sand needed to come up to a height of at least 2-inches, but not more than $^3/_4$ the length of the cone.

What is the minimum height of each of the cones?

E. 3 inches

F. $4^1/_2$ inches

G. $5^1/_3$ inches

H. 7 inches

NEED A CLUE? Imagine putting some arbitrary amount of sand in one [point down] cone. We can say that the height that the sand reaches is H, and the volume of the sand as V. Now picture adding sand so that the height of the sand is doubled to 2H, resulting in a volume that can be expressed as 2^3V or 8V.

Reminder: The formula for the volume of a cone (V) is:

$$V = \frac{1}{3}\pi r^2 h$$

Recreation and Sports Questions

(The answers for these questions can be found on page 99.)

43. Steve, Steve, Steve, Mary and Steve

Five friends, Steve, Steve, Steve, Mary and Steve go to a baseball game. One of them catches a foul ball. What are the odds that it was a Steve?

A. 5 to 1 in favor   C. 4 to 1 in favor
B. 1 to 5 in favor   D. 1 to 4 in favor

44. Team Player

Daniel plays soccer on a team in the local BES ("Busy Every Saturday") soccer league. There are 10 players on his team. At any one time, eight players are on the field. The coach always chooses his players randomly. What percent of the time does Daniel not play?

45. Round Robin

In a soccer league, there are 10 teams. They play in a round-robin tournament, where each team plays each of the other teams. Each time a team wins, it gets three points. For each tie, the team gets one point. For a loss, the team gets zero points.

After six weeks of play, the top four teams are the Cantaloupes, the Zebras, the Armadillos and the Beavers. Their standings are:

Rank	Team	Points
1	Cantaloupes	21
2	Zebras	17
3	Armadillos	15
4	Beavers	14

Assume the Cantaloupes don't lose any of their last three games. They only win or tie. Is it possible for the Beavers to win with the most points?

46. Batting Average

Joe Slugger is on the Mudville Nine baseball team. With 200 times at bat, Joe has a batting average of .250. Batting average is equal to the number of hits divided by the total number of times at bat. Of his next 100 times at bat, how many hits does Joe need to bring his batting average up to .300?

47. Play Ball!

Ryan and Jeremy finished playing their first two baseball games of the season. Their statistics for these games were:

	Ryan		Jeremy	
	Hits/ At Bat	Batting Average	Hits/ At Bat	Batting Average
Game 1	3 for 7	.429	1 for 2	.500
Game 2	1 for 4	.250	2 for 7	.286

Who has a higher batting average for the season?

48. Cracking the Lock

Lance rode his bike to the store. He wanted to keep it safe, so he brought along his bike lock. It had a combination lock with four wheels on it, and each wheel has the numbers 0 through 9. If you put the wheels in the correct order, the lock opens.

Now, Lance has a bad memory, so to help him remember the combination he used only even numbers 2, 4, 6 and 8, without duplication. Lance also put them in random order. Of course, Lance has forgotten the combination. What are the most combinations Lance will have to try to open the lock?

49. Slam Dunk

Sixty-four basketball teams have reached the playoffs. Each team plays until it loses. Teams continue to play until only one team remains. What's the fewest number of games that need to be played to determine the winner?

50. Super Sprinter

World-class sprinter Allyson Fleetfeet can run the 100-meter dash in about 10 seconds. If Allyson could maintain that pace for an entire marathon (26 miles and 385 yards), about how long would it her take to finish?

A. around 10 minutes
B. around 1 hour
C. around 3 hours
D. around 6 hours

51. Perfect Scores

Match the perfect score with the sport:

A) 300	1) Cross country
B) 180	2) Bowling
C) 15	3) Baseball
D) Shut out	4) Darts

52. Tennis, Anyone?

The serve of a professional tennis player can travel between 120 mph and 150 mph. Sally is just learning to play, so her serve travels at only about 80 mph (120 feet per second). A serve that can't be returned is called an ace. Typically, an ace will travel about 80 feet to land right in the corner of the court. If Sally hits the tennis ball on her serve when it is seven feet off the ground, what would be the best trajectory for her to try to achieve?

A. A positive slope (ascending)
B. A slope of zero (moving horizontally)
C. A negative slope (descending)

53. Triple Doubles

In Monopoly, you roll two dice and move the number of spaces equal to the sum of the dice. If you roll doubles, you get to roll again. However, if you roll 3 doubles in a row, you go directly to jail, do not pass Go and do not collect $200. What are the chances of this happening?

A. 1 in 6 C. 1 in 216
B. 1 in 36 D. 1 in a million

NEED A CLUE? First, determine the chances of rolling doubles on the first roll.

Economics Questions

(The answers for these questions can be found on page 111.)

54. Scrimp and Save

Right or Wrong: Your dad has agreed to help you save for a baseball bat. The bat costs $100. Your dad has offered to add 10% to whatever you save. You work hard and earn $90. Now, with your dad's contribution, you have enough money for the bat.

55. A Good Investment

As an employee of Dim Bulb Industries, you have an opportunity to invest some of your hard-earned money into one of their investment plans. The way their plan works is that every five years, the Dim Bulb financial advisors select three investments from which you can pick. Your return on the investment is governed by an equation that is a function of what year (Y) of the five-year cycle it is. Here are equations for the growth of the investments. Which choice provides the best rate of return?

A. Linear Growth: $35Y$
B. Cubic Growth: Y^3
C. Exponential Growth: 2^Y

56. Realty Check

Three realtors open an office together. After some length of time they each put up a poster showing their success at selling houses. All three charts represent accurate data over the same time period. If you were going to sell your house and use one of the three realtors, based on their sales chart, which one do you think would be the best pick?

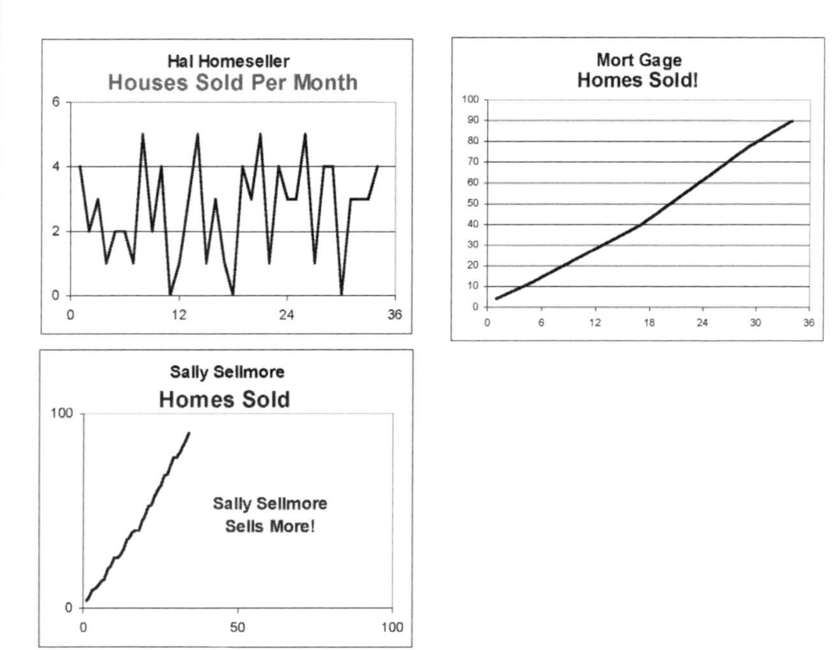

57. Examining eCommerce

Julio has been saving up all year to buy the newest video game system, PONG 8000. Being a good consumer, Julio has done his research on pricing before he gives up his hard-earned money. In the end, there are three stores where he is considering making his purchase. Ohms Emporium is a local store while OverWhelmed.com and We Sell the World are online businesses. Based on the following table, which is the best deal?

Store	Price	Discount	Tax	Shipping & Handling	Delivery Time
Ohms Emporium	$ 260	-	10%	-	pick up
Over Whelmed.com	$ 255	-	-	$ 25.00	5-7 days
We Sell the World	$ 250	5% (online only)	10%	$ 20.00	2-3 days

58. Chuck the Woodchuck

Giles notices an advertisement in the newspaper for an in-store discount of 50% off Woodchuck Chuckin' Wood. This is good news for Giles, who knows precisely how much wood his woodchuck Chuck chucks, since his woodchuck can chuck wood. At the store, Giles notes that Chuck's favorite flavor of Chuckin' Wood (maple, of course) has a coupon for an additional 50% off the lowest marked price. The cashier says that 50% + 50% = 100%, so the bag is free. Is the cashier correct?

59. DVD Deals

Ebony goes shopping for a new DVD. Luckily for her, the Dandy Dave's DVD Shoppe is having a sale. Buy one DVD and get 20% off, buy two and each DVD is 30% off, buy three or more and each DVD is 40% off. Ebony sees five DVDs she likes, but realizes she only has a $25 gift card to buy the DVDs. When making her selections, Ebony must remember the 5% tax and the $1.50 fee that will be taken from her gift card each time she uses it. Using the table, find the most DVDs Ebony can purchase while keeping within her $25 budget.

Movie Title	Price
Rabbit Fire	$15
Ro.Go.Pa.G.	$15
Le Notti Bianche	$20
The Crowd	$20
Day of Wrath (The Director's Cut)	$25

60. Peanut Whiz Kid

In Gooberville, grocery stores are required to list on the shelves not only the price per item, but also a unit price. The unit price helps the buyer figure out quickly which package of a certain product is the better deal.

One day Ellerína goes to SavClub to buy Peanut Whizzes. Next to each other on the shelf, she sees the Gooberville Greats brand that goes with the first label.

Next to it, she finds the Groovy Gill's brand with this label:

Which brand is the better price?

NEED A CLUE? Look for a mistake that was made on one of the unit price labels.

61. We All Scream for Ice Cream

Ogg and Nahtogg go to RocksCo to pick up a 55-gallon drum of their favorite ice cream (Rocky Road, of course). They plan on opening an ice cream shop, where they will sell 4-oz. scoops of ice cream for 50¢ each. They pay $220 for the ice cream and nothing for the ice cream cones (because they won't be invented for another 10,000 years, at the 1904 St. Louis World's Fair). If they sell all their ice cream, how much profit will they make?

A. They will lose money
B. $180
C. $660
D. $1100

62. Here's a Tip

In Gooberville, there is a tax of 7% on food sold in a restaurant. It is also customary to give a gratuity (also called a tip) to show your appreciation for the service. Typically, a good tip is between 15% and 20% of the total before the tax is added.

Bill
Food: $28.40
Tax: $2.00
Total: $30.50

Buffy goes to a restaurant. Her bill comes to $28.50, and the tax comes to $2.00. Estimate a tip between 15% and 20%.

A. $4.50–$5.00
B. $6.00–$7.50
C. $10
D. None of the above

63. Buying Tires

Farmer Kabibble needs to get new tires for his truck. At the tire store, he finds that there are two different-sized tires that would work. The Super Deluxe Dirt Grabbers are 60 cm in diameter, and the Premium Road Grippers are 50 cm in diameter. The price of the Premium Road Grippers is 10% less than the price of the Super Deluxe Dirt Grabbers. Which tires are the better deal?

64. Calling Card

Mary has a telephone calling card. The first minute costs $1.00 and all subsequent minutes or fractions of minutes cost 10¢. At the motel where Mary is staying, it costs $5 per day to make all the local calls she wants. Mary plans to stay one day and make three local calls that will last 8 to 10 minutes each. Should she use the local phone service or her calling card?

65. Interesting Interest

You have $100 in a bank account earning 2% interest per year compounded annually. If the interest rate never changes and you never add any more to the account, about how long will it take until you have $200 in your account?

A. 5 years C. 36 years
B. 16 years D. 50 years

66. Gaging a Mortgage

Consuela has decided to buy the purple house at 1999 Alphabet Street. Her realtor at Prince Properties, Nelson Rogers, has negotiated a purchase price of $200,000. After her down payment, she will need to borrow $167,000 from the Bank of Gooberville. This is a 30-year fixed rate mortgage with monthly payments and an annual interest rate of 6% (in this case, interest is the money she pays the bank for the use of the money).

Each month, Consuela will pay the bank $1,000. A portion of each payment is used to pay the interest she owes the bank, and the remaining money goes to reduce the loan balance. This is called "amortizing the loan." At the end of 360 months (30 years), the last payment will reduce the loan balance to zero, and Consuela will own the house outright. About how much interest will Consuela end up paying over the life of the loan?

A. $ 10,000 C. $100,000
B. $ 50,000 D. $200,000

NEED A CLUE? The easiest way to think about this is to calculate how much Consuela will pay total, and then subtract the portion that repays the principal. The principal is the amount of money that she owes the bank at any given moment.

67. Where Credit is Due

Ogg has just received his first MasterRock credit card ("Don't leave your cave without it!"). In the first month, Ogg charges way more money than he can afford. His charges equal $1,000, mostly iRock downloads. MasterRock tells him that he needs to make a minimum payment of 2% of the balance each month, but no less than $10.00. However, for every month after the 1st month, he will have interest added to his bill in the amount of 1.5% of the outstanding balance. Ogg decides not to charge any more until he pays off the entire bill. Assuming Ogg pays only the minimum each month, about how long will it take Ogg to off his balance?

A. 1 year C. 10 years
B. 5 years D. 20 years

68. Goody Goody Gumballs

You are buying gumballs for the gumball machine. You can either get 850 large gumballs for $50 or 8,500 small gumballs for $100. You can sell the large gumballs for 25¢ each and the small gumballs for 5¢ each. You have $100 to spend. Which type of gumballs should you buy to maximize your profit?

A. The big gumballs C. It doesn't matter
B. The small gumballs

69. Kabibbleberry Jam

Farmer Kabibble is selling jars of Kabibbleberry jam. He guesses that if he set the price at $4.00 that he could sell 120 jars. He thinks that every $1.00 increase means he would sell twenty fewer jars. On the other hand, for every $1.00 decrease, he could sell twenty more jars. If the goal is to maximize his revenue, what price should he charge?

A. $3.00 C. $5.00
B. $4.00 D. $7.00

Nature, Music & Art Questions

(The answers to these questions can be found on page 129.)

70. Nanoseconds

Rear Admiral Grace Murray Hopper (1906–1992) was a U.S. computer scientist and naval officer. She is famous for her nanoseconds visual aid. People (such as generals and admirals) used to ask her why satellite communication took so long, so she started handing out pieces of wire. The length of each piece of wire was the distance that light travels in one nanosecond.

Knowing that light travels at about 186,000 miles per second, about how long were Admiral Hopper's "nanoseconds"?

A. About one inch C. About one yard
B. About one foot

71. The Symmetry of Shapes

Let's say you have an image, and that you can rotate that image around some point. If, as you rotate the image, there are times when the image looks identical (when the rotation angle is less than 360°), the image has rotational symmetry at these times. For example, consider an equilateral triangle. Every time the triangle is rotated 120°, it matches up with the original shape:

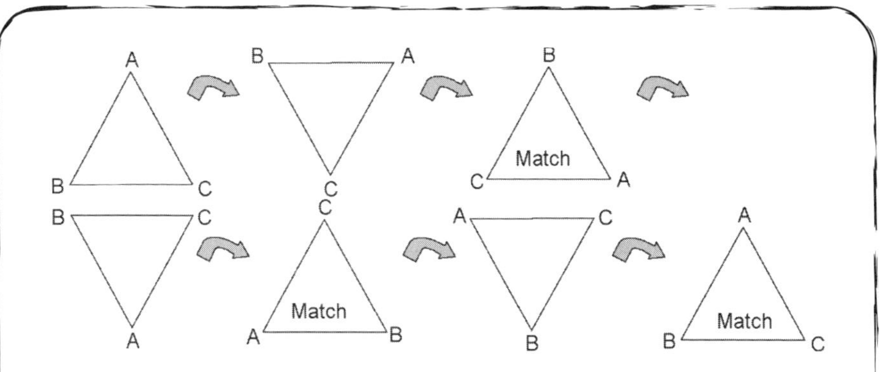

Because the shapes match up three times as the triangle rotates one complete revolution (360°), the triangle is said to have "rotation symmetry order 3".
Shapes in nature can also have rotational symmetry. What is the order of rotational symmetry for each of these objects?

A.

C.

B.

72. Abby's Birthday

Abby was born on Monday, July 21, 1997. When was the next time her birthday fell on a Monday again?

73. Scale Model

Michael Angelo has been commissioned to create a bronze sculpture. Before he builds the full-size sculpture, he builds a $^1/_{10}$th-scale solid bronze model. The model weighs two pounds. When the full-sized solid bronze sculpture is finished, will Michael be able to carry it himself?

74. Bubba the Flying Squirrel

The southern flying squirrel has a maximum glide ratio of 3:1. This means that it can glide about three horizontal feet for every vertical foot it falls.

Bubba the flying squirrel climbs to the very top of a 75-foot-tall hickory tree. While nibbling on the hickory nuts, he notices a cute squirrel on a tree 60 feet away and 40 feet below him. In an all-out attempt to impress the cutie, Bubba jumps and glides right to her. What glide ratio did Bubba use?

A. 3:1 C. 2:1
B. 3:2 D. 4:3

75. Naked Mole Rats

Most queen naked mole rats have average litters of about 11 baby naked mole rats, but some have been known to have 27 babies in a single litter. In a certain hive in sub-Saharan Africa lived a queen naked mole rat that was known to have had around 900 babies over 12 years of being queen. Given what we know, estimate how many litters a year this prolific queen had.

A. 2–4 C. 6–8
B. 4–6 D. 12-16

76. Terrific Tessellation

A tessellation is created when a shape is repeated over and over again covering a plane without any gaps or overlaps.

Think of tiles on a floor. Only three regular polygons (shapes that have the same length sides and interior angles) can tessellate a plane. Which of the following cannot?

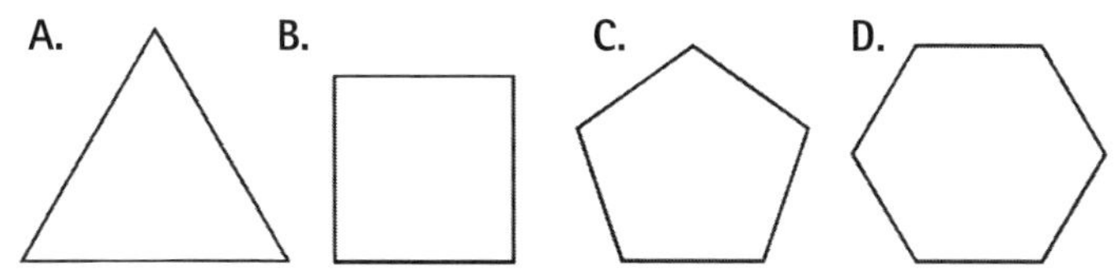

77. Map Quest

You have been challenged to color the map of the United States so that no two adjacent states are colored the same. States that touch at only one corner, such as Utah and New Mexico, are not considered adjacent. What is the fewest number of colors you need to use to win the challenge?

A. 3 C. 5
B. 4 D. 6

78. Patching Things Up

Jackie and Rachel need fabric to complete their quilt. Jackie buys a quarter of a yard (9" x 44") of fabric, while Rachel buys a "fat quarter" (18" x 22") of fabric. Both want to cut the fabric efficiently so that they have as many finished $3\ ^1/_2$" x $3\ ^1/_2$" squares as possible. When sewing fabric together, it's important for quilters to leave a $^1/_4$" seam, so the girls add $^1/_2$" when they cut their fabric. Who will cut the most squares?

79. Tag, You're It

Scientists like to keep track of the number of animals in the wild, especially endangered species. Since actual counting of individual animals is impossible, scientists have developed statistical methods to come up with valid estimates.

One method scientists use to count animal populations is to capture a few animals, identify them with tags and then let them go. Then after a while, they capture a few animals again and see how many have tags.

On one such counting mission, the scientists capture 10 Addax—desert antelopes found in the Sahara—and tag them. Two weeks later they again capture 10 Addax and find that one of them has been tagged. What do the scientists conclude?

A. There are around 20 addax in the wild
B. There are around 100 addax in the wild
C. There are at least 1,000 addax in the wild
D. Addax are easy to catch in the wild

80. Speed of Sound

Look at the chart, and use interpolation to find the speed of sound at 16,000 feet.

A. 750 mph   C. 718 mph
B. 720 mph   D. 701 mph

Altitude	Speed of Sound
0	761
1,000	758
5,000	748
10,000	734
15,000	721
20,000	706
25,000	693
30,000	678
35,000	663

NEED A CLUE? One of the simplest methods of interpolation is linear interpolation (sometimes known as lerp). Generally, linear interpolation takes two data points, say (x_a, y_a) and (x_b, y_b), and the point (x, y), called the interpolant. This is a point in between the other two. Typically x is known and y is solved for. The formula to solve for y is:

$$y = y_a + \frac{(x_b - x_a)(y_b - y_a)}{(x_b - x_a)}$$

81. Make a Pitch

Here's a formula about sound and ultimately about music: $v = \lambda f$, where v is the speed of sound, λ (the Greek letter lambda) is the wavelength of the sound wave, and f is the frequency of the sound wave.

Jonathan plays middle C on the piano. He then plays the note C one octave up, which is higher in pitch (frequency) than middle C. Is the wavelength of the second note longer or shorter than middle C?

82. Tuning Up

Benjamin is tuning his piano. He measures the frequency of each note. He finds that the note A above middle C is tuned perfectly at 440 Hertz (Hz). He knows that in music, an octave is the interval between one musical note and another with half or double the frequency. In other words, the same note an octave higher would have double the frequency, and a note an octave lower would have half the frequency.

The A an octave above plays at a frequency of 900 Hz and the A an octave below plays at 200 Hz. In terms of percent error, which note is more in tune?

A. The A an octave below
B. The A an octave above
C. They are both in tune
D. They are equally out of tune

83. Musical Mathematicians

Who on the following list of mathematicians (and who relied on math in their careers) also played a musical instrument?

A. Pythagoras
B. Albert Einstein
C. Enrico Fermi
D. Augusta Ada Byron, Countess of Lovelace
E. All of the above
F. None of the above

NEED A CLUE? Whenever you think math, think music.

84. Shapely Structures

Architects and engineers have used mathematical shapes to inspire their creations. Can you match the object with its inspiration?

A.

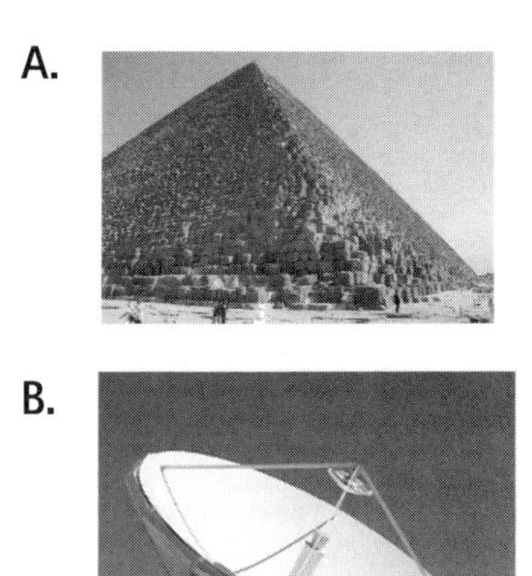

B.

C.

D.

1) arch
2) paraboloid
3) prism
4) square pyramid

85. The Big Chill

The equation to calculate wind chill (T_{wc}) is:

$$T_{wc} = 35.74 + 0.6215T_a - 35.75V^{0.16} + 0.4275T_aV^{0.16}$$

where T_{wc} and T_a (air temperature) are measured in °F, and velocity (or wind speed) in mph. Which line on the graph represents wind chill as a function of wind speed when air temperature is 20° F?

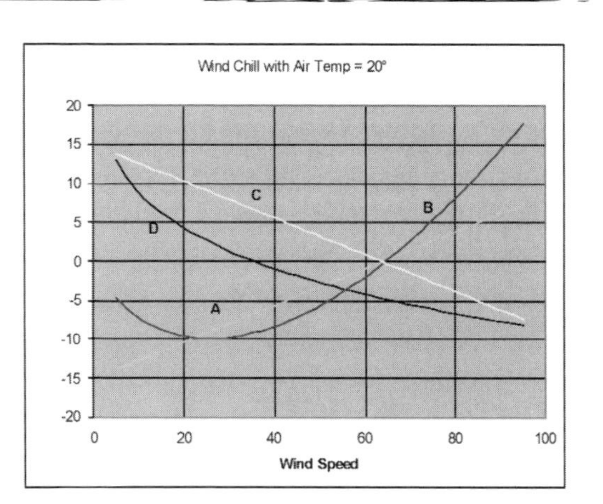

86. Watch for Falling Rocks

Two cavepeople, Ogg and Nahtogg, play a game in which they climb up on a cliff and drop rocks on the stuff that floats down the river. They know that, to hit a moving target, they have to drop the rock before the item is directly below them. They have been doing this so long that they have created a chart of how long it takes rocks to fall. When they climb up 100 feet, it takes 2.5 seconds for the rock to hit the object. How long does it take for the rocks to hit the objects if they climb up 400 feet?

A. 3 seconds C. 5 seconds
B. 4 seconds D. 6 seconds

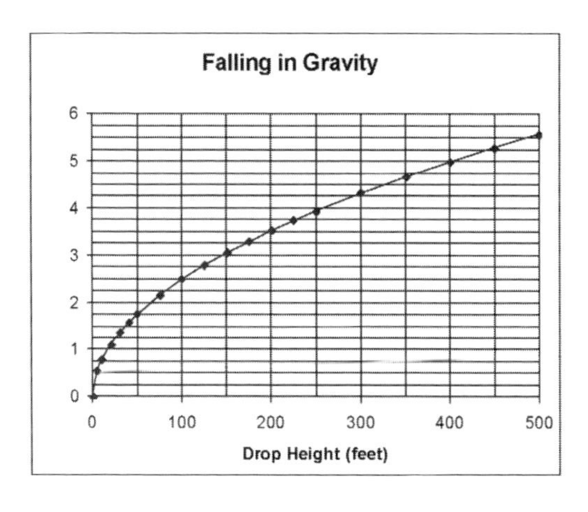

87. Shaking Things Up

Geologists use the Richter Magnitude Scale to compare the size and severity of earthquakes. The 1994 Northridge, California Earthquake was measured to be 6.5 on the Richter scale. The largest earthquake on record, the 1960 Great Chilean Earthquake, measured 9.5. About how much stronger was the Chilean earthquake?

A. 3 times stronger C. 100 times stronger
B. 10 times stronger D. 1,000 times stronger

88. Around the Sun

Which travels faster, the earth relative to the sun or the moon relative to the earth?

Hint: The earth is about 93 million miles from the sun, the moon is about 240,000 miles from the earth and pi is about 3.14.

89. Seeing the Light

The primary colors for light are red, green and blue. The secondary colors (made by mixing two primary colors) are yellow, cyan and magenta. In light, to get yellow, you mix red and green. To get cyan, you mix blue and green. To get magenta, you mix red and blue.

Red, green and blue lights create the colors you see on a computer screen. The intensity of each color is rated from 0 to 255, where 0 is no light and 255 is full on. This is called the RGB scale, where R stands for red, G stands for green, and B stands for blue. In the RGB scale, the color white is R=255, G=255, B=255; black is R=0, G=0, B=0; red is R=255, G=0, B=0; yellow is R=255, G=255, B=0 and so on.

In HTML (the computer language used to create web pages), each color is identified in a special RGB format: #rrggbb. In this format, the first two digits after the #

represent the intensity level for the red light, the next two digits represent the intensity level for the green light and the last two digits represent the intensity level for the blue light.

The intensity range is from 0 to 255, but the RGB format only leaves two digits for each color. How do we cram a three-digit number into two digits? We need to convert the decimal value for color intensity into base 16 (hexadecimal, or hex) (See question 97 for more on different number bases). In this number system, the "ones" place can hold the values 0 through 15 (base 10). The next place to the left is not the "tens place" as in base 10, but the sixteens place (because this is base 16—get it?) Now how do we put a 15 into the ones place? There are only 10 numbers developed for base 10 (0, 1, 2, 3, 4, 5, 6, 7, 8, 9). So, we improvise; we use letters. See the table below:

Base 10	0	1	2	3	4	5	6	7	8	9	10	11	12	13	14	15
Base 16	0	1	2	3	4	5	6	7	8	9	A	B	C	D	E	F

Match the RGB color code on the right with the most appropriate name on the left:

A. #8B4513 — 1. aqua
B. #800080 — 2. dark red
C. #FFD700 — 3. orange
D. #FFA500 — 4. gold
E. #8B0000 — 5. purple
F. #00FFFF — 6. brown

Miscellaneous Questions

(Answers to these questions can be found on page 151.)

90. Cave Paper

Ogg the caveperson wants to decorate a cavern in the cave by putting up wallpaper. From floor to ceiling, the cavern is 8 feet tall.

Conveniently, the cavern is rectangular; except one wall is completely gone (it's the entrance.) The long walls are 15 feet, and the remaining short wall is 10 feet. The mud-colored wallpaper Ogg buys at Cave Depot is 3 feet wide, and each roll is 20 feet long. Assuming Ogg doesn't care if there are horizontal seams, how many rolls need to be purchased?

91. Cave Paper Continued

Interestingly enough, Nahtogg, the other caveperson, has a cavern the exact same size. Nahtogg also wants to wallpaper the cavern with the exact same kind of wallpaper as Ogg (actually, the choice of wallpaper is not surprising because it is the only kind Cave Depot carries).

The difference is that Nahtogg is very particular and does not want any horizontal seams in the middle of her walls. If a strip of wallpaper is not at least 8 feet long, she plans to throw it away. How many rolls of wallpaper does Nahtogg need to purchase?

92. Pet Pen

Mal builds a rectangular pen to hold his pet snails. Then Mal decides to make one side of the pen longer by $^1/_3$. By what percentage should Mal reduce the other dimension to keep the area of the pen the same?

93. Weather or Not

Your mom tells you to pack for a surprise adventure. The one hint she gives you is to pack the type of clothes suitable for a place where the daytime temperature will be about 30°C. What should you pack for your afternoon adventure?

A. Tank tops and light pants or shorts
B. Flannel shirts and jeans
C. Wool sweaters, corduroy pants and a warm jacket

94. Temperature Crossover

The boiling point of water is 100°C or 212°F. The freezing point of water is 0°C or 32°F. Is there a temperature value that is the same on both the Celsius and Fahrenheit scales?

95. Flip a Coin

When your friend is bored, he has a habit of flipping a coin into the air, catching it and calling out whether it landed on heads or tails. Today, he is bored. You have heard him call out "Heads, tails, tails, heads, heads, heads." He then says to you, "I just flipped three heads in a row. What is the chance that my next flip will be heads?" Is it...

A. 25%   C. 75%
B. 50%   D. 100%

96. Betting on the Square

Barnabas is taking a timed math test, without a calculator. He comes to the last problem: 36^2. Barnabas is very slow doing multiplication with more than one digit, and he has less than one minute left. Do you think he will be able to solve the last problem in the time he has left?

97. Covering All the Bases

Match these multiplication problems with the base number system they were calculated in:

A. 4 x 4 = 20	1) Base 16 (hexadecimal)
B. 4 x 4 = 16	2) Base 12 (duodecimal)
C. 4 x 4 = 14	3) Base 10 (decimal)
D. 4 x 4 = 10	4) Base 8 (octal)

98. Exceptional Student Combinations

Every day in math class, the teacher picks the Exceptional Student of the Day and puts the name in a bowl. Each Friday the teacher picks 2 names out of the bowl for a prize. If your name is on both tickets, you get a homework pass that gives you the privilege of not doing one homework assignment. At the end of the first week, there are 5 names in the bowl and 2 of them are yours. What are the chances of you getting the homework pass?

99. Too Much Tunafish

Baozhai has a new digital music player, called a pPod. He puts 100 of his favorite songs on it. Baozhai chooses the function so that his pPod will play the songs in random order. Baozhai is concerned when out of the first 10 random songs, the song "Tunafish" is played three times. What should Baozhai do?

A. Put in a new battery
B. Add more songs
C. Return to the store for a replacement
D. Nothing—it is working fine.

100. Electoral College

The Electoral College is charged with electing the President and Vice President of the United States. Each of the 50 states is allocated electoral votes equal to the number of representatives in Congress (number in the House + the number in the Senate). The District of Columbia also has 3 electoral votes. There are 435 Representatives + 100 Senators + 3 DC votes = 538 total electoral votes.

As a rule of thumb, the electors from each state all vote for the Presidential candidate who had the most votes in their state. Whichever candidate has at least 270 electoral votes is elected president. This chart shows the number of electoral votes per state:

State	Electoral Votes	State	Electoral Votes	State	Electoral Votes
Alabama	9	Kentucky	8	North Dakota	3
Alaska	3	Louisiana	9	Ohio	20
Arizona	10	Maine	4	Oklahoma	7
Arkansas	6	Maryland	10	Oregon	7
California	55	Massachusetts	12	Pennsylvania	21
Colorado	9	Michigan	17	Rhode Island	4
Connecticut	7	Minnesota	10	South Carolina	8
D.C.	3	Mississippi	6	South Dakota	3
Delaware	3	Missouri	11	Tennessee	11
Florida	27	Montana	3	Texas	34
Georgia	15	Nebraska	5	Utah	5
Hawaii	4	Nevada	5	Vermont	3
Idaho	4	New Hampshire	4	Virginia	13
Illinois	21	New Jersey	15	Washington	11
Indiana	11	New Mexico	5	West Virginia	5
Iowa	7	New York	31	Wisconsin	10
Kansas	6	North Carolina	15	Wyoming	3

What is the fewest number of states required to reach 270 electoral votes?

A. 6 C. 16

B. 11 D. 26

101. Census Consensus

As of the last census, the town of Gooberville has 855 people, 367 households and 230 families residing in the town. The population density was 842.2/mi^2 (323.6/km^2). There were 411 housing units at an average density of 404.8/mi^2 (155.6/km^2). There were 678 dogs, 300 cats and 104 birds owned as pets. Based on this information, which one of these statements is true?

A. Gooberville is larger than one square mile

B. Every household in Gooberville owns at least one dog

C. There are no people that live alone in Gooberville

D. Every family owns at least one cat

Bonus Questions

(The answers for these questions can be found on page 164.)

1. Monthly Lunch

A group of 7 friends go out to lunch every month. All the friends pay for their own meals, unless it is someone's birthday that month. The birthday boy or girl does not pay to eat because the rest of the group pays for his or her meal. Their favorite restaurant has a large selection of lunch specials that all cost the same. With tax and tip, each person pays exactly $12.00.

At one such lunch, the friends noticed that certain months don't have any birthdays, some only have one birthday, and some have two or more birthdays.

One friend also noted that the people who don't share their birthday month pay more money in the course of a year than those who do share their birthday month. What formula should be used to be sure that, over the course of a year, each person pays the same amount?

2. Freedom the Frog

Freedom the frog has a peculiar habit. When he jumps, he can leap halfway across the room. But when he makes his next leap, he leaps only half the remaining distance, and with the next leap, again, jumps only half the remaining distance. Given enough time, will Freedom ever make it out of the room?

3. Counting in Binary

Ogg the caveperson is in charge of keeping track of the tribe's collection of rocks. This is an important responsibility, so Ogg is working on a way to keep a running count of the rocks. The problem is that writing has not yet been invented, so the only way Ogg has to keep a record is by counting on his fingers. If the tribe starts out with 837 rocks, what is the fewest number of hands Ogg needs to start tracking the 837 rocks?

4. Road Trip

Ella and her family are going on a car trip. They plan to visit the towns neighboring Gooberville, her home town. Using the map and mileage chart, plan a route that starts and ends in Gooberville, requires the least amount of driving, and will take Ella and her family to each of the other towns only once.

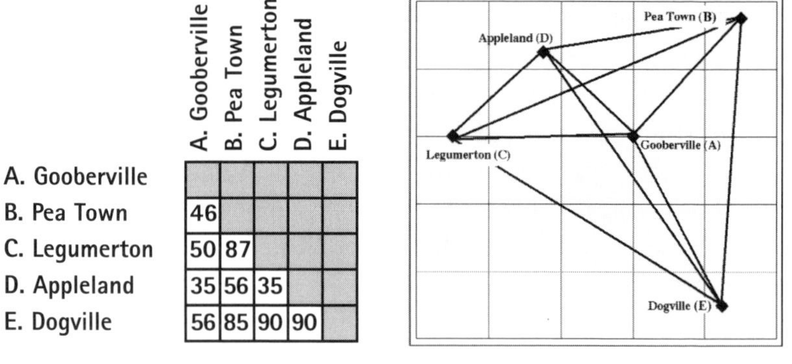

	A. Gooberville	B. Pea Town	C. Legumerton	D. Appleland	E. Dogville
A. Gooberville					
B. Pea Town	46				
C. Legumerton	50	87			
D. Appleland	35	56	35		
E. Dogville	56	85	90	90	

5. Funny Bunnies

Leo read an ad in Cabin Foci Weekly about rabbits. The ad said that if you buy one pair of newborn rabbits, then

1) They become fertile in two months.
2) Once they are fertile, every month they will become parents of a new pair.

Before you know it, Leo is the proud owner of a pair of newborn rabbits. Here's how time progresses:

- At the beginning of the 1st month, he has one pair.
- At the beginning of the 2nd month, he still has one pair.
- At the beginning of the 3rd month, just as the ad said, there are now two pairs of rabbits.
- 4th month, the first pair gives birth to another pair making three pairs.
- At the beginning of the 5th month, Leo counts 5 pairs of rabbits, and realizes the set born in the 3rd month must have given birth as well.

Leo makes a chart to figure out how many pairs of rabbits he will have at the end of the year:

Beginning of Month Number	Number of Pairs
1	1
2	1
3	2
4	3
5	5
6	
7	
8	
9	
10	
11	
12	

How many pairs will there be at the end of the year?

DOWNLOADING ANSWER.
ESTIMATED TIME REMAINING 04:14
241
+359
GLASBERGEN

Facts, Just Math Facts Answers

1. Easy as Pi

On March 14th, Albert's school celebrated Pi Day. They had several pi-related events, including a pie sale. What was the price of each pie?

- **A. $1.43**
- **B. $2.31**
- **C. $3.14** ☜
- **D. $4.44**

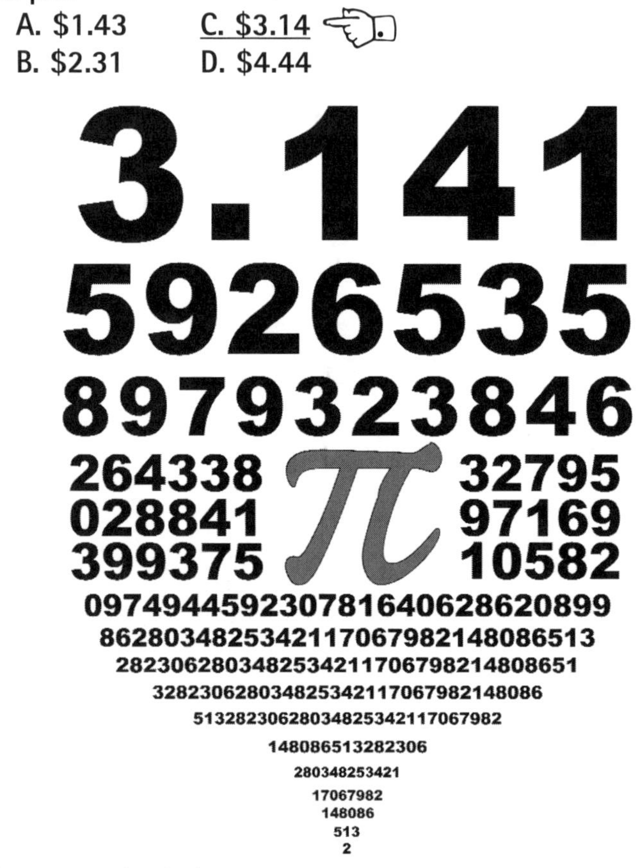

The answer is: C, $3.14

$3.14 is a good answer since the value of pi is approximately 3.14. Swiss mathematician Leonhard Euler named this special number pi after the Greek letter. You can calculate pi by dividing the circumference of a circle, any circle, by its diameter. The answer will always equal 3.14.

Since 1987, people have been celebrating Pi Day on March 14. People also celebrate Albert Einstein's birthday on the same day. He was born March 14, 1879.

Hmm! Pi (π) was proven to be irrational in 1761 by Johann Heinrich Lambert. A number is considered irrational if it can't be expressed as one whole number (also known as an integer) divided by another whole number. In other words, if you write the number in decimal notation, it never ends and it never repeats. Computers have calculated π out to 16 billion decimal places, just to be sure. So, why is it important that π is irrational? It makes a difference in advanced math.

You can use either 3.14 or the fraction $^{22}/_{7}$ as good approximations when you need to estimate the value of π.

2. Hip To Be Squared

What is the square of 15?

HINT: The square of a number is that number multiplied by itself. Its notation is a superscripted '2'; a number x squared is written as x^2. For example, the square of 3 is written as 3^2 ($3 \times 3 = 9$). The square of 14 (14×14) is 196, and the square of 16 (16×16) is 256.

The answer is: 225

Here's the fastest way to solve this problem: the hint told you that the answer must be between 196 and 256 (14^2 and 16^2). When a number that ends in the number 5 is squared, the result will always end in 25. Therefore, 15^2 must end in 25. There is only one number between 196 and 256 that has 25 as its last two digits: 225.

3. A Prime Number

Ogg, the caveperson, went hunting but didn't bring anything home. So, Nahtogg sent him to the butcher to buy some prime rib. Ogg returned with 4 bags of rib bones, each one containing a different quantity:

Bag A: 2 ribs **Bag C: 4 ribs** ☜

Bag B: 3 ribs **Bag D: 5 ribs**

Nahtogg complained, "I send you to store for prime rib. One bag not prime rib, but composite rib. Go back to store and get all prime rib!"

Which bag made Nahtogg cranky?

NEED A CLUE? A prime number (also called a prime) is a whole number that has exactly 2 whole numbers (called "factors") that divide into it. The two factors are 1 and the prime number itself.

The answer is: Bag C, 4 ribs

The first 30 prime numbers are 2, 3, 5, 7, 11, 13, 17, 19, 23, 29, 31, 37, 41, 43, 47, 53, 59, 61, 67, 71, 73, 79, 83, 89, 97, 101, 103, 107, 109 and 113. All primes are positive, and 2 is the only even prime number.

A number that is not a prime is called a composite number. This means that it has more than two factors. Four, for example, is divisible by 1,4, and 2, and is a composite number.

Zero and 1 are the only exceptions since they are neither prime nor composite.

4. Following Orders

Solve the following: $7 \times 3 + 2 \div 4 - 2^2 \times (6 - 1)^2$

NEED A CLUE? The key to this problem is understanding which calculations you need to do first, a technique called "order of operations." In arithmetic and algebra, problems like the one above are evaluated using a universal set of operations.

These precedence rules are used in many computer programming languages and modern calculators. However, they are only tools that help you arrive at the answer and are not math "facts."

The answer is: -78.5

What is the order of operations?

1. Parentheses
2. Exponents
3. Multiplication and division
4. Addition and subtraction

An easy way to remember the order of operations is to use a mnemonic (pronounced NEW-mon-ick): "Please Excuse My Dear Aunt Sally," or PEMDAS. A mnemonic device is a word or phrase that helps you remember information.

In an arithmetic problem, you calculate the expression inside the innermost parentheses first, and work outward.

Next, do all the exponents and roots. Stacked exponents must be done from right to left. The radical symbol (√) acts kind of like parentheses to group everything that is within them together.

Then, do all the multiplication and division, from left to right.

Finally, do all of the addition and subtraction, from left to right.

In this case:

$7 \times 3 + 2 \div 4 - 22 \times (6 - 1)^2 = 7 \times 3 + 2 \div 4 - 22 \times 52 = 7 \times 3$
$+2 \div 4 - 4 \times 25 = 21 + {}^1/_2 - 100 = -78.5$

5. Given the Choice

What is the result when you multiply 107 by 23?

A. 1,811 **C. 2,461** ☜
B. 1,986 **D. 2,593**

NEED A CLUE? Usually, when multiple answers are provided (as in this case), you can rule out one or two of the answers very simply. One of the easiest ways is to figure out whether the answer should be odd or even.
If the numbers are both odd, then the answer will be odd. Otherwise, the answer will be even.

The answer is: C, 2461

In this case, 107 and 23 are both odd, so their product is also odd. So we can rule out answer B, which is even. That leaves three possible answers.

Next, if we multiply the ones digits of each number together we get 7 x 3 = 21. The ones digit of this product (1) will be the ones digit of the answer. So now we can rule out answer D.

Now we can try to estimate the answer. We can round 107 to 100 and 23 to 20 and then multiply them together: 100 x 20. The product will be less than the real answer because we reduced both multipliers. Therefore we know that the answer must be at least 100 x 20 = 2000.

Of our two remaining choices (A or C), only one satisfies this condition so the answer must be C, 2461.

Estimating works pretty well for multiple-choice answers. Next time you need to know the precise answer, grab a pencil and paper!

6. You Know the Drill

Joe has a $^3/_8$" wire that he needs to thread through a hole in a piece of wood. He wants the hole to be as small as possible, but still allow the wire to easily go through. His drill bits are all in metric units (millimeters). Which is the best drill bit to use?

A. 5 mm **C. 15 mm**

☞ **B. 10 mm** **D. 20 mm**

The answer is: B, 10 mm

Find it fast! Here's how to estimate:

To convert from inches to millimeters, you must multiply the inches by 25.4. For our purposes we can start by rounding the conversion factor to 25. Next we have to multiply $^3/_8$ by 25. 25 divided by 8 is a little more than 3 and 3 x 3 = 9 so a 10 mm hole would be a good size. You can prove this to yourself with a calculator: $^3/_8$" = 9.525 mm.

7. Find it Fast

What is the product of 25 x 19?

The answer is: 475

Find it fast! You could just multiply.

Or here are two strategies that you might find faster:

1. Recognize that 19 = 20 – 1. Then we can imagine the problem as 25 x (20-1) = 25(20) – 25(1) = 500-25 = 475.

2. Imagine that instead of the equation 25 x 19, what you actually have is 19 quarters. The question then looks like: How many dollars do you have? Well, to convert from quarters to dollars you would divide the 19 by 4 and get 4.75. But a quarter is 0.25 and we want it to be 25, so we multiply our answer by 100 and get 475.

8. Facts and Figures

Match up each geometric figure on the left with its correct name on the right.

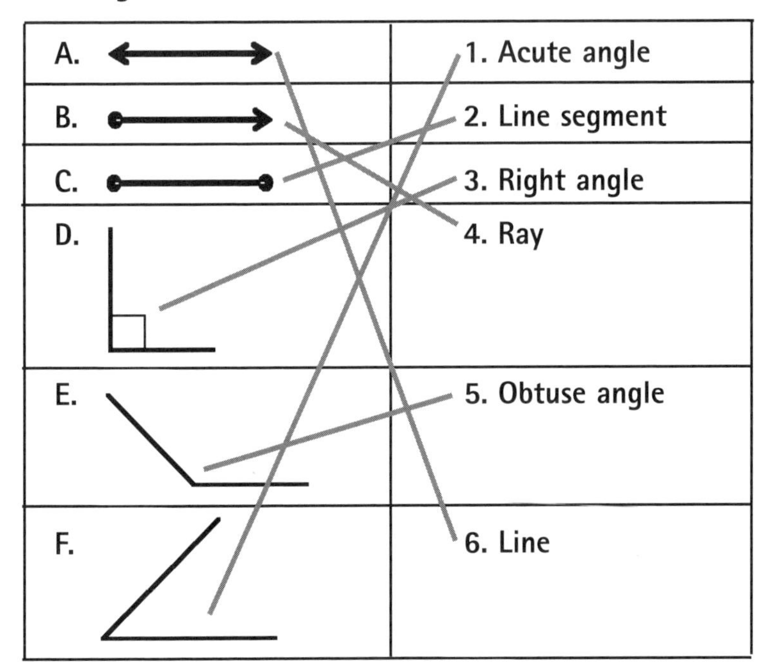

Geometry (from the Greek words geo, meaning "earth," and metria, meaning "measure") is the field of mathematics dealing with spatial relationships. Those are the relationships between points, lines, angles, surfaces and solids. To be able to describe both the real and theoretical worlds it is important to be able to distinguish between different types of lines and shapes.

For instance:

- A simple line always extends off to infinity in both directions.
- A ray extends in only one direction. Think of a ray of light that originates at one point and keeps going forever.
- A segment is only a part of something, so a line segment is only a portion of a line and terminates at both ends.
- Angle measurement is based on how much of a circle the angle uses. A circle always measures 360° around (If you want to know why, ask the ancient Babylonians). If you measure only half way around the circle, the semicircle would measure 180°.
- If you measure half way around the semicircle, the resulting angle would equal 90° and is called a right angle.
- An obtuse angle is any angle that measures greater than 90°.
- An acute angle measures less than 90°.

9. Name That Polygon

A polygon (from Greek, meaning "many-angle") is a set of line segments, in the same plane, that connect end to end. The straight line segments that make up the polygon are called its sides or edges and the points where the sides meet are the polygon's vertices, or corners.

Here are the names of polygons with varying number of sides, from 3 sides to 10 sides. Put the names of the polygons in order from fewest sides to most sides.

A. Decagon
B. Octagon
C. Triagon (Triangle)
D. Pentagon
E. Heptagon
F. Nonagon
G. Hexagon
H. Tetragon (Quadrilateral)

The answer is: C, H, D, G, E, B, F, A

In case you ever need to impress someone with your knowledge of geometry, here is a list of the names of some more polygons:

Sides	Polygon		
11	Hendecagon		
12	Dodecagon		
13	tridecagon or triskaidecagon		
14	tetradecagon or tetrakaidecagon		
15	pentadecagon or quindecagon or pentakaidecagon		
16	hexadecagon or hexakaidecagon		
17	heptadecagon or heptakaidecagon		
18	octadecagon or octakaidecagon		
19	enneadecagon or enneakaidecagon or nonadecagon		
20	icosagon	90	enneacontagon
21	icosihenagon	100	hectagon or hectogon
30	triacontagon	1,000	chiliagon
40	tetracontagon	10,000	myriagon
50	pentacontagon	100,000	decemyrigon
60	hexacontagon	1,000,000	hecatommyriagon or hekatommyriagon
70	heptacontagon		
80	octacontagon	Infinity (∞)	Circle

10. Polygon Area

Put these regular geometric shapes in order of least to greatest area.

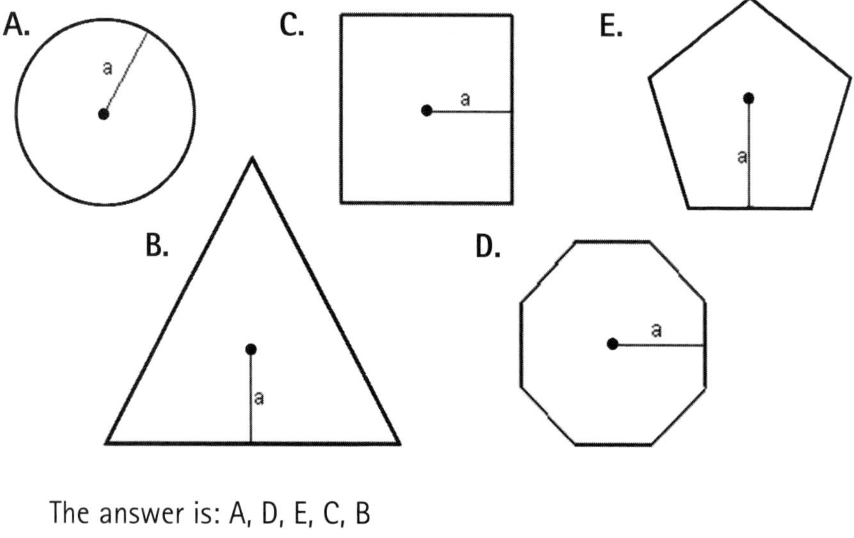

The answer is: A, D, E, C, B

The circle fits neatly inside each of these shapes. Notice that the more sides, the better the fit. All these polygons are superscribed about the circle.

The technical term for the distance from the center of a regular polygon to the midpoint of a side is called the apothem.

The formula for the area (A) of a regular polygon is $A = {}^1/_2\ ap$, where "a" is the apothem and "p" is the perimeter of the polygon.

HINT: The perimeter of a regular polygon can be calculated by multiplying the length of each side by the number of sides. The formula for this calculation is $A = {}^1/_2\ nsa$, where "n" is the nu--mber of sides, "s" is the length of each side, and "a" is the apothem.

11. Polygon Area, the Sequel

Put these regular geometric shapes in order of least to greatest area.

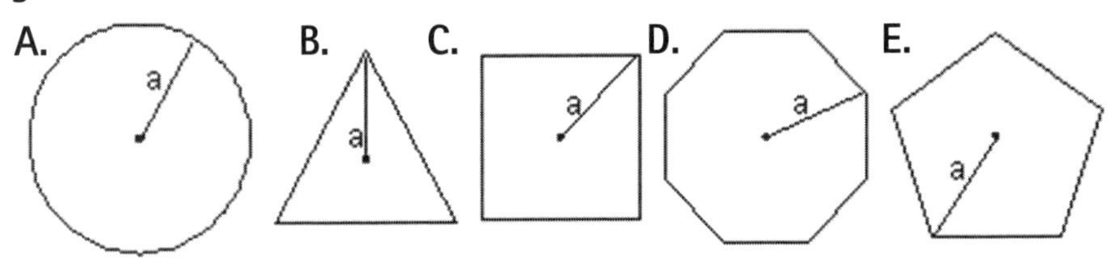

The answer is: B, C, E, D, A

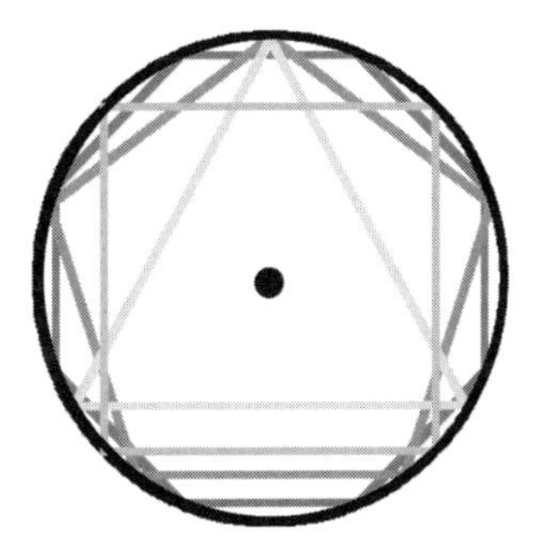

Here, we have the opposite situation from question 10. All of these shapes fit nicely inside a circle; and remember, the more sides, the closer the fit.

All these *polygons* are *inscribed* within the circle.

12. Show Me a Postcard

My 9th grade algebra teacher, Mr. Hronas, has a special picture frame that measures 3 feet by 2 feet. In it are postcards that students sent him from their vacations around the country. Each postcard is 4 inches tall by 6 inches wide, and none overlap. He can hang the frame either horizontally or vertically. What is the maximum number of postcards he can put in the frame?

The answer is: 36

If the frame is hung with the long side horizontal, then he could put 36" ÷ 6" = 6 postcards across and 24" ÷ 4" = 6 postcards down, for a total of 6 x 6 = 36 postcards.

On the other hand, if the frame turned 90°, so the short side was horizontal, then he could put 24" ÷ 6" = 4 postcards across and 36" ÷ 4" = 9 postcards down, for a total of 4 x 9 = 36 postcards.

13. The Great Pumpkins

As part of a science experiment, Habib is growing two pumpkins, each with its own special soil mixture. Every day, Habib weighs each pumpkin and measures its diameter. He needs to plot the data on a graph. Which of the graphs below should he use?

A.

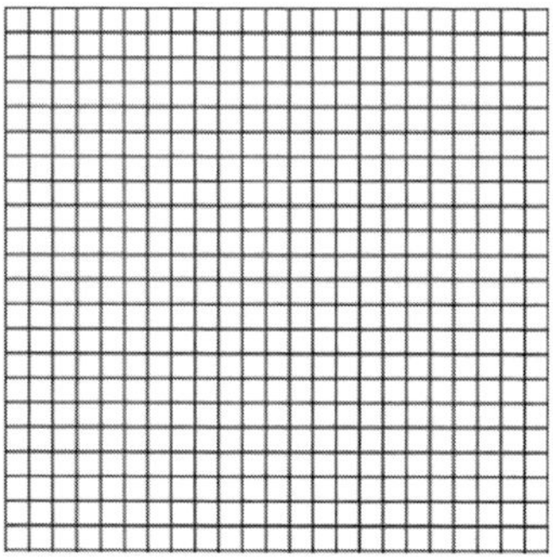

B.

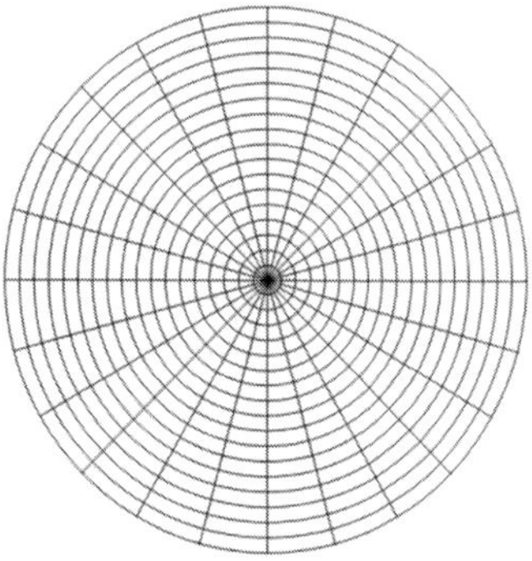

C.

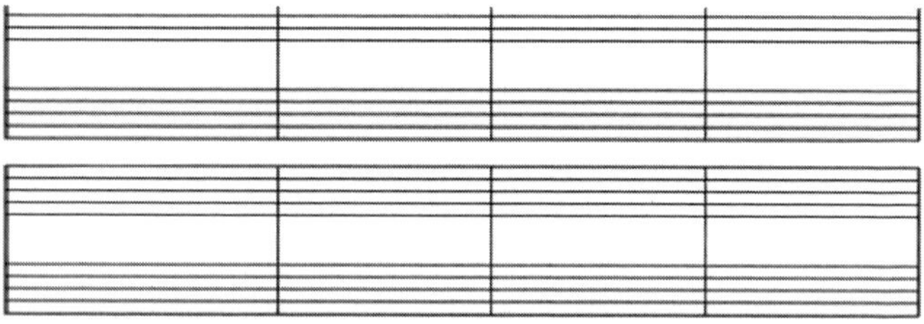

D.

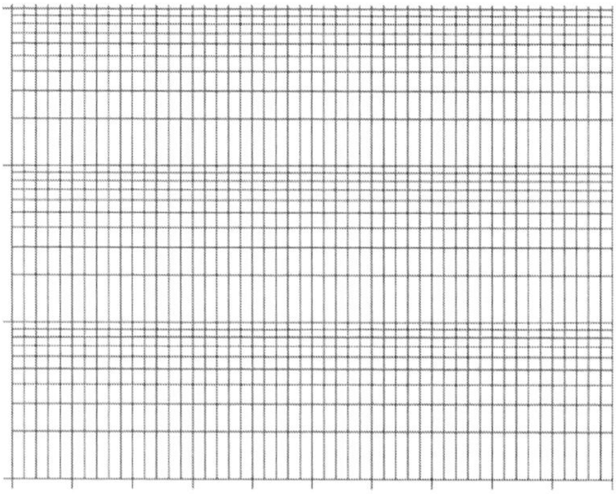

The answer is: A

A graph is a way for us to organize and display data that we can then use to learn.

Habib used (A), a "rectangular" grid called the Cartesian coordinate system. He put in the weight (x-axis) and diameter (y-axis) of the pumpkins as linear distances from a zero point in the center of the graph. It's a good way to see trends, such as the growth of the pumpkins. This sort of graph is named for the French mathematician and philosopher René Descartes, who published his ideas for it in 1637. It's used in physics, engineering, navigation, robotics, and, of course, mathematics.

In the polar coordinate system (B), the points are given by angle and a distance from a central point. It's good for plotting locations. You may have seen it on the radar displays that track airplanes.

A musical scale (C) is a way of graphing what notes to play and in what order and rhythm to play them.

A logarithmic scale (D) uses the logarithm of a physical quantity instead of the quantity itself. In other words, it allows us to represent a large amount of data in a smaller, more manageable range. The Richter magnitude scale, which measures the strength of earthquakes, is one example of a logarithmic scale. Others measure the loudness of sounds, the brightness of stars, and the pH (acidity or alkalinity) of substances.

14. Over the Moon

Spencer, the space cadet, is flying 1,000 meters over an airless moon at a speed of 30 kilometers per hour (kph). He drops a marker to remind him to visit that area again. From the viewpoint of someone standing on the moon, which of the following trajectories (paths) is the marker most likely to take on its way down to the surface?

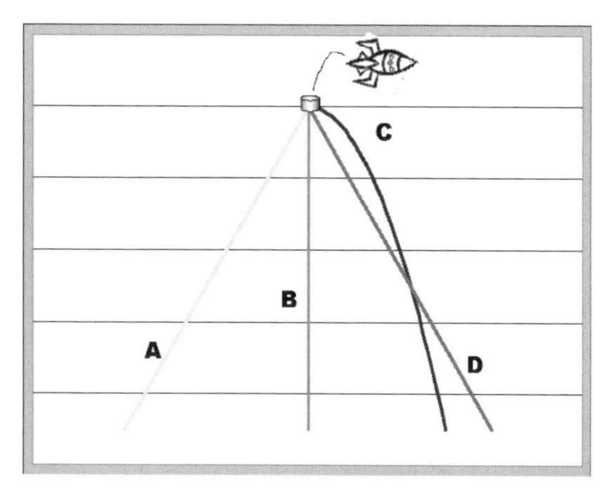

The answer is: C

There may not be any air on the moon, but it still has the pull of gravity. Two properties will affect the marker's path: gravity and forward motion (since Spencer's space ship was moving when he dropped the marker). Because Spencer was moving to the right, the marker did, too. This rules out path A and B. Gravity tends to make something that is falling go faster and faster as time goes on. That means that the path will curve. So, the answer is C.

15. Father of Algebra

Who is considered the father of algebra?

☞ <u>**A. Muhammad ibn Musa al-Khwarizmi**</u>
B. Euclid of Alexandria
C. Gottfried Wilhelm Leibniz
D. Leonhard Euler

NEED A CLUE? The source of the world "algebra" is an Arabic word: al-jabr

The answer is: A

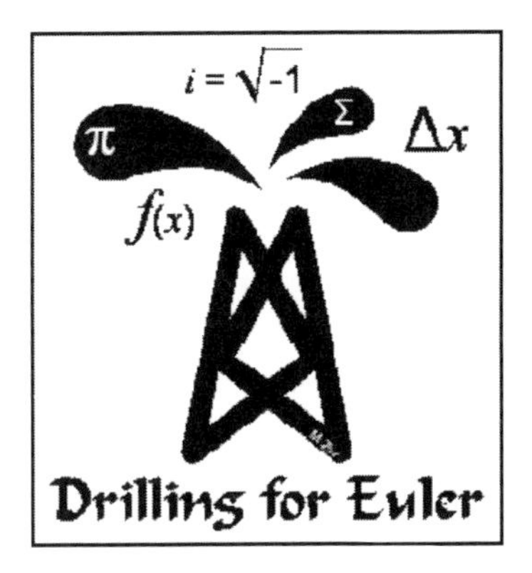

The word "algebra" comes from the title of Muhammad ibn Musa al-Khwarizmi book, Hisab al-jabr w'al-muqabala, written around the year 830 BCE. The title translates to "Calculation by Restoration and Reduction." Besides other important advances, al-Khwarizmi was among the first to use zero as a number. This probably seems simple, since you already know about zero, but imagine if you didn't! He's also immortalized in another way: the word "algorithm" is derived from his name.

Euclid is the "father of geometry." He was a Greek mathematician who lived in Alexandria, Egypt between about 325 and 265 BCE. His most popular work, Elements, is still widely-used today.

Gottfried Wilhelm Leibniz (1646-1716) was a German polymath (someone who excels in multiple fields). Leibniz is famous not just for his work in mathematics, but also for his contributions to philosophy, biology, medicine, geology, politics, psychology, theology and law. One of Leibniz's claims to fame is his invention of calculus. Sure, Isaac Newton usually gets the credit, but Leibniz invented calculus independently, and it is Leibniz's notation that is still used. He even developed the binary system, the foundation of virtually all modern computer architectures.

Leonhard Euler (pronounced "Oiler") (1707-1783) was a Swiss mathematician and physicist. He created much of the terminology and notation for mathematics, including the notations for square root and pi. According to the Guinness Book of World Records, he holds the record for mathematical authorship. His collected works fill 60 to 80 volumes. Euler is so famous that his picture is on money in Switzerland.

16. Proof Positive

True or false: the following proves that 1=2:

Suppose a = b	
Multiply both sides by b	$ab = b^2$
Subtract a^2 from both sides	$ab - a^2 = b^2 - a^2$
Factor both sides	$a(b - a) = (b + a)(b - a)$
Cancel (b – a) from both sides	$a = b + a$
Substitute a for b, since a = b	$a = a + a$ or $a = 2a$
Divide both sides by a	$1 = 2$

The answer is: False

When we cancel factors, we are actually dividing by that factor. If $a = b$, then $b - a = 0$. We can't divide by zero so the proof is false.

So just what is a proof? A proof is a logical way of proving something is true. It starts with a hypothesis. It proceeds, step by step, based on what we know to be true (called "theorems") and what we assume to be true (called "axioms"). If every step of the argument is true, then the conclusion must also be true.

Another way to use a proof is instead of proving something to be true, we can assume it's false and see if we can arrive at a contradiction.

Health, Food & Nutrition Answers

17. Pi and Pie

Since Albert loves pie, he planned on trying many kinds of different pies at his school's Pi Day celebration. The only problem is that Albert's mother told him he could eat no more than the equivalent of a quarter of a pie. Albert had enough money to purchase as many slices as he wanted. However, he had difficulty making his choices because not all the pies were cut into the same number of slices.

Type of Pie	Number of Slices per Pie
Strawberry	6
Apple	8
Cherry	10
Chocolate Cream	10
Banana Cream	12
Lemon Meringue	12
Boston Cream	16
Coconut Cream	16

What is the maximum number of slices of different pies Albert can buy so that he ends up with no more than the equivalent of $^1/_4$ of a pie?

NEED A CLUE? Start by choosing the pies that have the most slices per pie. These slices will be the smallest.

The answer is: 3

Start with the pies with the smallest slices. The Boston Cream and the Coconut Cream pies each have 16 slices, so one slice of each pie would total $^2/_{16}$ of a pie, or $^1/_8$. The next smallest slices come from the Banana Cream and Lemon Meringue pies at 12 slices per pie. Adding the two slices already picked and one more slice from a 12-slice pie is $^1/_8 + {}^1/_{12}$.

In order to add these fractions together we need to make the denominators (the bottom numbers) the same. We can do that by finding the least common multiplier for 8 and 12. Relying on our math facts, we know that both 8 and 12 are factors of 24 so $^1/_8 + ^1/_{12}$ becomes $(^1/_8) \times (^3/_3) + (^1/_{12}) \times (^2/_2) = ^3/_{24} + ^2/_{24} = ^5/_{24}$, which is less than $^4/_{24} = ^1/_4$. Since there are no pies sliced into 24 pieces, Albert can have a maximum of 3 slices.

18. Smart Cookie

Inara is having a party and is going to make her famous Alphabet Cookies. To make sure everyone will get a cookie, she will make one and a half batches. Everything is going well until the recipe calls for $^1/_3$ cup of butter. Inara only has measuring cups in the following denominations: $^1/_8$ cup, $^1/_4$ cup, $^1/_3$ cup, $^1/_2$ cup & 1 cup.

Can Inara measure out the correct amount of butter using her measuring cups?

The answer is: Yes

If Inara doesn't have a measure for $^1/_2$ the original amount of butter ($^1/_2 \times ^1/_3 = ^1/_6$ cup), maybe she has a measure for 1 $^1/_2$ times the original amount. To figure this out, we can express what we need as fractions ($^3/_2 \times ^1/_3$). The 3 in the numerator (the top part) of the first fraction cancels the 3 in the denominator (the bottom part) of the second fraction. That leaves us with the fraction $^1/_2$ cup, for which Inara has a measuring cup.

19. Half-Baked

Inara is having another party and is going to make her famous Alphabet Cookies again, but this time she wants to make only half a batch. Everything is going well until, yet again, the recipe calls for $^1/_3$ cup of butter. Inara still only has measuring cups in the following denominations: $^1/_8$ cup, $^1/_4$ cup, $^1/_3$ cup, $^1/_2$ cup & 1 cup.

Can Inara measure out the correct amount of butter using her measuring cups?

The answer is: Yes

Once again, Inara does not have a $^1/_6$ measuring cup. This time, she has a more creative solution. First, she measures out $^1/_2$ cup of butter. Then, she uses her $^1/_3$ measuring cup to scoop out $^1/_3$ cup of butter from the $^1/_2$ cup. The amount that remains in the $^1/_2$ cup is $^1/_2 - ^1/_3 = ^3/_6 - ^2/_6 = ^1/_6$ cup.

20. Tin Pan Tally

A cake recipe says to put batter into two 8" round pans, but you don't have any. Of the following, which combination of pans will work best?

A. Two 8" square pans
B. One 9" square pan
C. One 9" x 13" rectangular pan
☞ **D. Three 8" x 4" rectangular pans**

The answer is: D, three 8" x 4" pans

Here's how to figure it out:

- The area (A) of an 8" round pan is: $A = \pi r^2 = \pi 4^2 \approx {}^{22}/_7(16) \approx 50$ in^2, so two pans have a combined area of about 100 in^2.
- Two 8" square pans have a combined area of $2 \times 8^2 = 128$ in^2.
- One 9" square pan has an area of $9 \times 9 = 81$ in^2.
- One 9" x 13" pan has an area of $9 \times 13 = 117$ in^2.
- The combined area of three 8" x 4" pans = $3 \times (8 \times 4) = 96$ in^2.

Therefore, the three 8" x 4" pans provide the area closest to 100 in^2.

21. Marshmallow Treats

A recipe calls for 5 cups (about 72 cubic inches) of large marshmallows. Unfortunately, you only have mini marshmallows. All the marshmallows are perfect cylinders. The large ones have a *diameter* of 1-inch and are 1-inch in height. The mini marshmallows are $^1/_2$ inch in *diameter* and $^1/_2$ inch in height. If you measure out 5 cups of mini marshmallows into a rectangular pan measuring 8" x 9" x 1" and you don't squish the marshmallows in, are you most likely to have:

A. A larger volume of marshmallows

B. A smaller volume of marshmallows

☞ **C. The same volume of marshmallows**

The answer is: C, the same volume of marshmallows.

We can place one large marshmallow in each square inch of the pan. When we do that there is some space left void. The amount left void is the area of the square minus the area of the circle. $A_{void} = A_{square} - A_{circle} = 1^2 - \pi r^2 = 1 - \pi\,(^1/_2)^2 = 1 - \pi/4 \approx 1 - {}^3/_4 \approx {}^1/_4$ in^2. This means that when we inscribe a circle inside a square, 25% of the area is left void. If we calculate the same thing for the small marshmallows, we would place each small marshmallow within a $^1/_2$ inch square. In this case, $A_{void} = A_{square} - A_{circle} = {}^1/_2{}^2 - \pi(^1/_4)^2 = {}^1/_4 - \pi/16 \approx {}^1/_4 - {}^3/_{16} = {}^1/_{16}$ in^2. Again, the area left void is 25% of the area of the square ($^1/_4$ in^2 x 0.25 = $^1/_{16}$ in^2).

In fact, the percent of void space will be the same regardless the size of the square. From this we can conclude that it doesn't matter whether the marshmallows are large or small. Note: This is only true because the measuring container is sufficiently large compared to the marshmallows. If a standard 1-cup measure was used, then you would get more mass with the small marshmallows.

22. Putting on the Zits

Jordan is a teenager. Therefore, there is a 25% chance he will wake up each morning with at least one pimple. For Jordan, it takes two days for each pimple to go away. If Jordan has no pimples on Thursday, what are the chances that Jordan will have at least one pimple by Saturday night?

A. 0% **C. 88%**

☞ **B. 44%** **D. 100%**

NEED A CLUE? This one looks hard, but it is easier to figure out how likely it is for Jordan not to have any pimples. Here is the key: The exact opposite of having at least one pimple is not having any pimples.

The answer is: B, 44%

For Jordan to have a pimple on Saturday night, there must be a pimple either Friday morning or Saturday morning. The question says that the *probability* of having at least one pimple on Friday morning (or any morning) is 25%, so the *probability* of not having a pimple must be 75%. The same is true for having a pimple on Saturday morning. So, the *probability* of not having a pimple on Friday morning *and* not having one on Saturday morning is (75%)(75%) = .75 x .75 = .56 , or 56%.

But, remember, this is the answer to the opposite of what we want to know. Our answer is 1.00 - .56 = .44, or a 44% chance that Jordan will have at least one pimple by Saturday night. Where did this equation come from? If there are only two possible outcomes, then the *probability* of one of the outcomes is equal to 100% minus the *probability* of the other outcome.

23. Cricket Calories

While filming a reality TV show on a remote tropical island, you find yourself lacking enough calories to compete in the challenges. In the hope of surviving, you decide you must find something to eat, even if it isn't exactly to your usual tastes. There are plenty of insects on the island. Maybe you'd like to get the calories you need by munching on crickets.

How many calories are in 100 grams of crickets?

A. 1,727 calories

☞ <u>B. 121.5 calories</u>

C. 179.5 calories

Nutritional Value of Various Insects per 100 grams

Insect	Protein (g)	Fat (g)	Carbohydrate(g)
Giant Water Beetle	19.8	8.3	2.1
Red Ant	13.9	3.5	2.9
Silk Worm Pupae	9.6	5.6	2.3
Dung Beetle	17.2	4.3	0.2
Cricket	12.9	5.5	5.1
Large Grasshopper	20.6	6.1	3.9
Small Grasshopper	14.3	3.3	2.2
June Beetle	13.4	1.4	2.9
Caterpillar	6.7	N/A	N/A
Termite	14.2	N/A	N/A
Weevil	6.7	N/A	N/A

Data collected from The Food Insects Newsletter, July 1996 (Vol. 9, No. 2, ed. by Florence V. Dunkel, Montana State University) and Bugs In the System, by May Berenbaum

NEED A CLUE? Here's how to calculate how many calories you can get from insects: Calories = 4 x (carbohydrate + protein) + 9 x (fat), where carbohydrates, protein and fat are measured in grams

The answer is: B, 121.5 calories

To calculate the number of calories in 100 grams of crickets, use this formula: Calories = 4 x (carbohydrate + protein) + 9 x (fat).

Plug in values from the chart:

* First, put in the calories from carbohydrate and protein: $4(5.1 + 12.9) = 72$
* Then, put in the calories from fat: $9(5.5) = 49.5$
* Finally, add the two results: $72 + 49.5 = 121.5$ calories

24. Going Buggy

As you explore the island, you find there are alternatives to the crickets. You discover a large colony of red ants, a colony of termites and an endless supply of June beetles. Use the nutritional chart in question 23 to decide which will provide you with the most calories.

☞ A. Red ants   **C. June beetles**
B. Termites

NEED A CLUE? You can figure out this without any calculations. Look at the formula: Calories = 4 x (carbohydrate + protein) + 9 x (fat). Note that the amount of fat is the most important factor.

The answer is: A, red ants

Just compare the amounts of fat on the chart in question 23.Termites have no fat at all, and red ants have more than twice as much fat as June beetles. Therefore, the red ants will provide the most calories.

If you need to see the math to prove it to yourself, here it is: Using the formula: Calories = 4 x (carbohydrate + protein) + 9 x (fat) and plugging in the values from the chart we find the following:

Food	Calories
Red Ants	98.7
Termites	56.8
June Beetles	77.8

25. Pizza Combo

You've got 22 hungry football players back at the house, and you're out looking for pizza. Each player wants his own pizza, which consists of one kind of crust, one kind of cheese, and one topping. They don't care what they get as long as nobody gets the same pizza. You have three pizza parlors to choose from:

- **Mama Cass** – they've got 1 kind of crust, 1 kind of cheese and 18 different toppings
- **Tiddly's** – 2 kinds of crust, 2 kinds of cheese and 5 different toppings
- **Shack o' Pizza** – 3 kinds of crust, 3 kinds of cheese and 3 different toppings.

From which pizza place are you going to order the pizza?

A. Mama Cass

B. Tiddly's

☞ **C. Shack o' Pizza**

D. You're out of luck; none of the places can make what you need. You get to spend another year as the tackling dummy.

The answer is: C, Shack o' Pizza.

The way to determine the number of combinations is to multiply the options for each category.

- In the case of Mama Cass, there are 1x1x18 = 18 different pizzas.
- Tiddly's can create 2x2x5 = 20 different pizzas.
- Shack o' Pizza can create 3x3x3 = 27 different pizzas.

26. Pizza Combo Part 2

Apparently, one pizza wasn't enough. You are now being sent to the pizza parlor that can give you the greatest number of two topping pizzas (Each pizza must have two different toppings on it). Where are you going?

A. Mama Cass
B. Tiddly's
C. Shack o' Pizza
D. To another school that doesn't have such hungry football players

The answer is: A, Mama Cass.

This time, we have to select a second topping. In the case of Mama Cass, there are 1x1x18 = 18 different pizzas with 1 topping, but for each pizza, there are 17 choices for the second topping. Remember that we aren't allowed to repeat.

That means for Mama Cass, there are 1x1x18x17 = 306 different two-topping pizzas.

Similarly, Tiddly's can create 2x2x5x4 = 80 different two-topping pizzas.

Shack o' Pizza can create 3x3x3x2 = 54 different two-topping pizzas.

27. Dough Boy

Wolfgang is making bread. After he mixes the flour, water, yeast and all the other ingredients together, he has a four-cup glob of dough. He then puts the dough in a bowl, covers it, and puts it in a warm place to rise. After the dough doubles in volume, Wolfgang punches down the dough so it loses $^1/_3$ of its volume. He then allows the dough to double in size again, before he puts it in the oven to bake.

How big a bowl does he need so that the dough does not pop over the top or ooze over the sides?

A. 1 quart **C. $^1/_2$ gallon**

☞ **B. 6 pints** **C. 75 oz**

NEED A CLUE? Begin by figuring how many cups of dough there are after all the rising and punching and rising again. Then convert the cups to another kind of measurement.

The answer is: B, 6 pints

First let's figure out how big the dough grows:

It starts at 4 cups and then doubles to 8 cups.

It gets reduced by a third, which is $^8/_3$ cups = 2 $^2/_3$ cups. 8 cups – 2 $^2/_3$ cups = 5 $^1/_3$ cups.

The dough rises to twice its volume again and ends up being 5 $^1/_3$ cups x 2 = 10 $^2/_3$ cups. So the answer is... hmm, none of the answers is in cups.

We will have to convert.

One quart = 2 pints = 4 cups, so A is out.

There are four quarts in a gallon, so half a gallon is 2 quarts, or 8 cups. So, C is not big enough.

Next, there are 8 oz in a cup, so $^{10}2/_3$ cups is 8 $(10+^2/_3)$ = 80 + $^{16}/_3$ = $85^1/_3$ oz. That leaves D out as well.

One pint = 2 cups, so 6 pints = 12 cups. Twelve cups are bigger than $^{10}2/_3$ cups. Therefore, B is the solution.

28. Sugar and Spice

Farmer Kabibble is famous for his hot chocolate. When he makes a cup for himself he uses $1^1/_3$ tablespoons of unsweetened cocoa powder; 3 tablespoons of sugar; $^1/_2$ teaspoon of the Farmer's special spices; and 1 cup of a super secret blend of milk, cream, vanilla and boiling water.
The local high school has asked Farmer Kabibble to make a 100 cup vat of his hot chocolate so they can sell it as a fundraiser at their football game.

How much cocoa powder will Farmer Kabibble need to make 100 cups of his famous hot chocolate?

A. $3^1/_2$ cups	**C. $8^1/_3$ cups** ☜
B. $5^3/_4$ cups	**D. 10 cups**

The answer is: C, 8 1/3 cups

This is pretty straightforward. There are $1^1/_3$ tablespoons of cocoa in one cup, so Farmer Kabibble needs 100 $(1^1/_3)$ = 133 $^1/_3$ tablespoons for the fundraiser. Now we just have to convert to cups:

There are 16 tablespoons in a cup so we divide $133^1/_3$ by 16. Don't let this scare you! The first thing to notice is that 16 times 10 is 160, which is larger than 133, so D is not the answer.

Half of 160 is 80 (which is 16 x 5), and 80 is much too low, so B and A are out.

That leaves C. Ta-da!

29. Hard Pill to Swallow

Each morning Xander must take a pill containing 100 mg of medicine. Let's assume that the medicine is immediately introduced into his system. Among other things, our bodies work to wash foreign stuff out, including medicine. Because of this process, in 24 hours, Xander's body will wash out 40% of the existing amount of medicine in his body. Xander takes his medicine at 8:00 a.m. each morning. If he takes it for the first time on Monday, how much medicine is in his body just before he takes his dose on Wednesday?

A. 64 mg **C. 128 mg**

☞ **B. 96 mg**

The answer is: B, 96 mg

On Monday, just after taking the dosage, Xander has 100 mg of medicine in his system. On Tuesday, just before taking the second dose, he has 60% of 100 mg (60 mg) of medicine in his system. Just after taking the Tuesday dose, he has 160 mg in his system. On Wednesday, just before taking his daily dose he has 60% of 160 mg, which is 96 mg.

30. Worth the Wait

The body mass index (BMI) is a formula designed to identify the relative weight range of a person based on the person's height. The accepted range for good health is 18.5 to 25. The formula for body mass index is:

$$\text{BMI} = \frac{\textbf{weight (kg)}}{\textbf{height x height (m x m)}}$$

It was formulated in metric units (kg/m^2). However, in the United States, we typically use pounds to measure weight and inches to measure height. If we use these units to measure BMI instead of the metric units, then the BMI tables have to be altered. Will using pounds and inches cause the best BMI range numbers for good health to be higher or lower?

The answer is: Lower.

Think about it:

- 1 kg is equal to about 2.2 pounds, so that would make the range move up to values that are a little more than double the metric values.
- On the other hand, in the denominator, we see that height is squared. And, 1 meter is equal to about 39 inches. So, in the denominator is the number 392, or 1521. You can round 1,521 up to 1,600 if you like, since the actual number isn't necessary to answer the question.
- So, the new BMI range is a little more than doubled. Then, you divide the numerator value by 1521.
- The effective change is to divide each value by about 700, so the range becomes 0.026 to 0.036, which is lower than the original range.

Of course, these numbers are hard to remember, so BMI is always expressed in metric units. To convert the English units to metric, simply multiply by 703 (this is the actual, not an estimated, scale factor between the English and metric units).

Notice that the question only asked whether the numbers would be larger or smaller, not for an actual number. Therefore, estimates of the numbers are good enough.

Travel Answers

31. Dim Bulb Racing

Dim Bulb Racing Promoters Inc. has organized an airplane race around the world. To make sure the pilots don't get in each other's way, they have planned for each plane to start on the same longitude line, but on different latitude lines. The pilots must stay on their own latitude lines throughout the race. You will fly in the race. By random drawing you are the first to choose the latitude line on which you will fly. Which of the following latitudes will you pick?

A. 45°S **C. 30°N**
B. 0° **D. 60°N** ☜

NEED A CLUE? Remember that latitude lines run east to west, parallel to the Equator (latitude 0°). All longitude lines run between the North and South poles. They all intersect each other at the two poles. The line of longitude that is designated at 0° is called the Prime Meridian. An easy way to remember the difference is to think of latitude lines as rungs on a ladder. Think of longitude lines as long.

Lines of Latitude

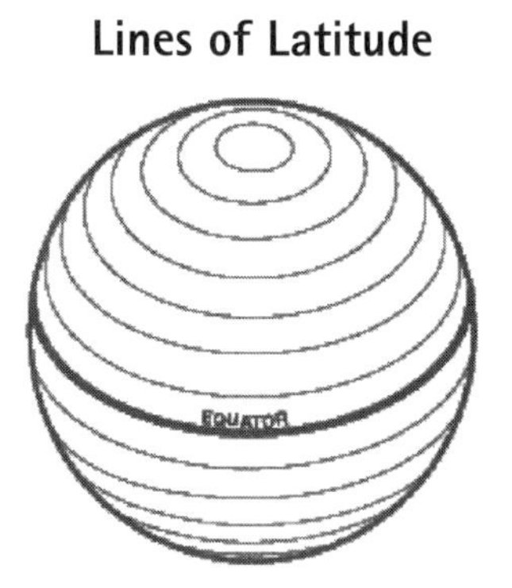

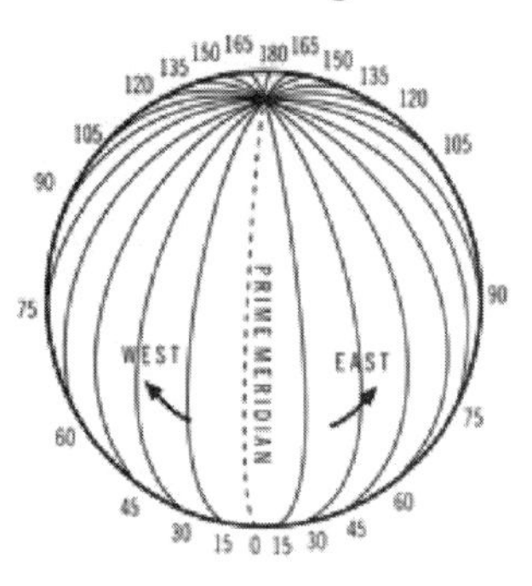

The answer is D, 60°N

As the lines of latitude get further from the Equator (latitude 0°), the radius of the circles get smaller and smaller. As the radius of each circle of latitude gets smaller, so does the circumference. So, the higher the angle of latitude (either north or south), the shorter the distance an airplane would have to fly to get all the way around the world and back to the starting point.

This means that latitude 60°N would be the smallest circle of the choices. If you fly that latitude in your airplane, you have the fewest miles to travel, and you're more likely to win the race.

32. Zoning Out

The continental United States has four time zones: the Pacific, Mountain, Central and Eastern Time Zones. There are 24 time zones around the world. If you were to estimate how many degrees of longitude enclose the continental US based on time zones, how many degrees would there be from California to Maine?

A. 5° to 25° **C. 60° to 90°**

☞ **B. 30° to 60°**

NEED A CLUE? There are 360° in a circle and 24 time zones defined for the earth. So, ideally, each time zone is made up of 360° ÷ 24 = 15° of longitude.

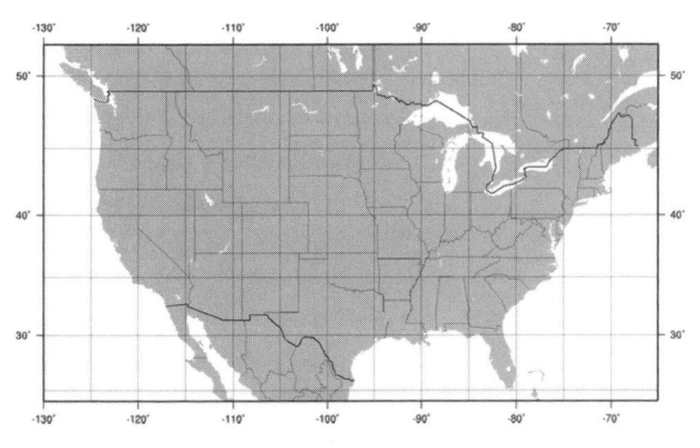

The answer is: B, 30° to 60°

There are 360° in a circle and 24 time zones defined for the earth. So, each time zone is made up of 360°÷24 = 15° of longitude. Since we don't know whether the US completely fills the four time zones or just barely enters them the range would be 4x15° = 60° as a maximum and 2x15° = 30° as a minimum.

Hmm! In 1878, to help with standardizing train schedules, Canadian Sir Sanford Fleming proposed a system of worldwide time zones. Since the earth rotates once every 24 hours and there are 360 degrees of longitude, each hour the earth rotates one-twenty-fourth of a circle or 15 degrees of longitude.

The entire United States stretches across six time zones, from east to west: Eastern, Central, Mountain, Pacific, Alaskan, and Hawaiian-Aleutian. For the most part, these time zones are one hour apart. This can get complicated, as not all states (or parts of states) observe Daylight Saving Time. Daylight Saving Time runs from the second Sunday in March (when people in most parts of the United States set their clocks ahead one hour) to the first Sunday in November (when they set their clocks one hour back).

33. Instantaneous Travel

Louise flies on a commercial airline from Louisville, Kentucky, to St. Louis, Missouri. As the plane takes off, she notices the time is 1:00 p.m. She has time for just a couple of Sudoku puzzles before the plane lands and the flight attendant announces, "Welcome to St. Louis, where the time is 1:00 p.m." Louise is convinced the flight attendant can't tell time, but sure enough, it is 1:00 p.m. in St. Louis. What happened?

The answer is: Nothing mysterious.

The flight from Louisville to St. Louis was an hour long. However, there is a time zone change. Louisville is in the Eastern time zone, while St. Louis is in the Central time zone.

34. Flying to Florida

Glen wants to fly from Los Angeles, California to Orlando, Florida to watch baseball spring training. His airline ticket looks like this:

From			To	
3/11	LAX	11:00 a.m.	ORL	7:00 p.m.
3/18	ORL	11:00 a.m.	LAX	1:00 p.m.

Glen notices that it takes 8 hours to fly from California to Florida, but only takes 2 hours to fly back. What's going on?

The answer is: Time zones

The flights actually take the same amount of time. Airlines report take-off and landing times based on each airport's local time zone. Los Angeles is in the Pacific Time zone, while Orlando is in the Eastern Time zone. The times in these zones are 3 hours apart. When Glen lands in Orlando at 7:00 p.m., it's 4:00 p.m. in Los Angeles, so taking off at 11:00 a.m. Pacific translates into a 5-hour flight. The apparent 2-hour return flight, when adjusted for the 3-hour time difference, is also a 5-hour flight.

35. Ticket to Ride

Maya rides the train to work every weekday and rarely takes a day off. During normal months, she can spend either $25 for 1 round-trip ticket, $70 for a pack of 5 round-trip tickets, or $240 for a monthly pass. In December, the rail line offers a 25% discount on the monthly pass. After working all year, Maya finally wants to take some time off in December. As it turns out, she will only be working 8 days that month. What combination of passes/tickets should she buy?

The answer is: Two packs of 5 round trips

You may think that two packs of 5 are not very efficient because she will not be able to use two of the tickets. But, review the table, and you can see that buying in bulk saves money.

8 Days	
Monthly Pass	\$240 x 0.75 (which is 100% – 25%) = \$180
2 Packs of 5	\$70 x 2 = \$140
1 Pack of 5 + 3 Single tickets	\$70 x 1 + \$25 x 3 =\$145
8 Single Tickets	\$25 x 8 = \$200

36. There and Back Again

Zach lives a mile from school. It takes him 15 minutes to ride his bike to school, but only 5 minutes to ride home (There's a lesson on motivation here, but that's beside the point). What is Zach's average speed?

A. 4 miles per hour **C. 8 miles per hour**

☞ **B. 6 miles per hour** **D. 12 miles per hour**

The answer is: B, 6 miles per hour

Distance is given in miles, and we want to know Zach's rate in miles per hour, or miles/hour.

If it takes Zach 15 minutes to go one mile to school and 5 minutes to come home, it takes Zach a total of 20 minutes to go 2 miles. That means Zach's average rate is:

r = 2 miles/20 minutes = 2 miles/($^1/_3$) hour = 6 miles per hour.

37. Get Me to School on Time!

You are riding your bike to school, which is 10 miles from your house. You know that you have to average 10 miles per hour to get to school on time. When you are half way there you realize you have averaged only 5 mph. How fast do you have to go on the remaining half of the trip to get to school on time?

A. 15 mph C. 30 mph

B. 20 mph D. You can't possibly get there on time

The answer is: D, you can't possibly get there on time

You can figure this one out with no calculations. Going half the distance at half the speed, you have taken just as much time as going all the distance in all the time. Forget the numbers in the problem for a moment.

The formula is this: Distance = Speed x Time.

If you reduce the speed to half, and cut the distance in half, then the time stays the same.

Multiply both sides of the equation by a and get $aD = aST \Rightarrow (aD) = (aS)T$. Notice that the time (T) doesn't change. If we let a = 0.5, we halve the distance and the speed. Once again, we can see that the time stays the same. That means that having gone half the distance at half the speed has used up all the time you had, and you can't avoid being late. Next time, you'll need to pedal faster, so eat an earlier breakfast!

38. Going the Extra Mileage

Jackie drives a new hybrid car that keeps track of the gas usage as miles per gallon (mpg). Jackie knows that the rate of gas consumption varies based on how fast she accelerates and whether she is going up or downhill. Usually, Jackie *averages* 50 mpg.

On one trip from her house to the beach 50 miles away, Jackie notices that she has only managed 40 mpg. Jackie decides she wants her *average* back up to 50 mpg. So, on the way home, following the same path, Jackie works to *average* 60 mpg, and does. However, when she arrives home she finds that her average gas usage for the whole day is not 50 mpg, but 48 mpg. Why?

The answer is: You need to use a different formula to average rates.

Averaging rates like miles per gallon (or miles per hour) is different from averaging test scores or ages. The key is that something like mpg is already an average. To figure out the gasoline burn rate over the course of a specific trip, you find the number of miles traveled and divide that by the gallons of gas used.

Jackie went 50 miles using fuel at a rate of 40 miles/1 gallon. What we need is a formula that leaves us with gallons but no miles. We get that by dividing the miles traveled (50) by the rate of fuel used (40): 50 miles/(40 miles/1 gallon) which becomes (50 miles x 1 gallon)/40 miles .

The miles cancel out and the fraction simplifies to $^5/_4$ gallon used for the trip to the beach. For the trip back Jackie got 60 mpg, and using the same formula we find that the gas used is 5/6 gallon. So, for the whole trip the average mpg is

$$100 \text{ miles}/(^5/_6 + {^5/_4}) \text{ gallons} = 100 \text{ miles}/\ ^{25}/_{12} \text{ gallons} = 48 \text{ mpg}.$$

Now, to figure out what Jackie's mpg goal should have been, we first need to know how many gallons Jackie needs to use over 100 miles to get 50 mpg.

100 miles/(50 miles/1 gallon) = 2 gallons.

During the first half of the trip, the car burned $^5/_4$ or 1.25 gallons.

So, to use a total of 2 gallons only (2 – 1.25) gallons or 0.75 gallons can be used for the second half of the trip.

The target mpg is then 50 miles/.75 gallon = 66.67 mpg.

39. Sprockets

Bob has a new mountain bike with three sprockets in the front and six sprockets in the back. Each sprocket, front and back, is a different size. Bob can use each possible combination of sprockets to make a "gear." Each gear gives him an advantage in speed or in riding up and down hills. How man different "gears" does the bike have?

The answer is: 18

This question is asking how many different ways you can combine the three sprockets in front with the six sprockets in back. You find this by multiplying the number of front sprockets with the number of rear sprockets: 3 x 6 = 18.

40. Moon Landing

The country of Grand Fenwick wants to explore several locations along the equator of the moon. They hire Dim Bulb Aerospace to build a rocket powerful enough to get to the moon. After the moon-lander touches down, the astronauts will explore the area and then move 100 miles along the equator to a new location.

Dim Bulb tells the Grand Fenwick Space Agency that to save money and complications, the moon-lander can't move sideways—just up and down. When the astronauts want to change locations, they must take off in the lander, hover above the surface as the moon rotates below, and finally land in a new location.

According to Dim Bulb's estimates, the circumference of the moon at the equator is 5,600 miles and the period of the moon (how long it takes to spin completely around once on its axis) is 28 days. If Dim Bulb's theory and numbers are correct, how long will the astronauts have to be off the surface of the moon to land 100 miles from where they started?

NEED A CLUE? If the circumference of the moon is 5,600 miles, then 100 miles would be $^1/_{56}$ of the distance around the moon. If it takes 28 days for the moon to fully spin around its axis, in one day it would travel $^1/_{28}$ of the way around. So you can figure that $^1/_{56}$ the circumference is half of $^1/_{28}$ the circumference.

The mathematical answer is: 12 hours

The astronauts will be off the surface for $^1/_2$ a day, or 12 hours.

But there's a problem.

Truth in advertising: The basic physics of the problem are wrong. When the moon-lander takes off from the moon, it is traveling at the same velocity as the moon is so it is also moving sideways. If the lander does not travel very far off the surface, then the astronauts would not notice the moon surface moving, at least not immediately.

Additionally, if the lander leaves the surface of the moon, it will continue moving in a straight sideways path, at constant velocity. The surface of the moon may appear to move sideways, but it is actually rotating while the lander is going straight. Therefore, in time, the astronauts would see the moon's surface fall away. In theory, leaving the surface straight up then coming down would work, but it would take much longer than the twelve hours calculated.

The other important thing to know is that Dim Bulb Aerospace has made some errors in its calculation of the size of the moon as well. The circumference of the moon at the equator is not 5,600 miles, but 6,553 miles; also, the moon's period is not 28 days but 27.3 days.

41. June Bugs

Stacey, Tracey, Macy and Clyde all play in a band called the June Bugs. They travel from one performance to the next in Tracey's van. The van gets 15 miles per gallon.

Their agent has lined up two possible gigs for them on Saturday night. One is at the City A Auditorium, pays $200 and is 15 miles away. The second possible gig is at the City B Bistro, pays $300 and is 150 miles away. Take into account that the agent will get 10% of the fee off the top (meaning they have to pay their agent first before expenses) and consider that gas costs $3 a gallon.

Which gig will be a better deal for the June Bugs?

The answer is: The City B Bistro

For the City A gig, they make $200.

- First, $20 ($200 x 0.1) goes to the agent.
- Then figure how much the gas costs for the round trip. $3 x (2 x 15mi) ÷ 15mpg = $6 for gas.
- That leaves $174.

For the City B gig they make $300.

- First, $30 ($300 x 0.1) goes to the agent.
- $3 x (2 x 150mi) ÷ 15mpg = $60 goes to gas.
- That leaves $210.

42. Around the World

When Ferdinand Magellan set off to be the first to circumnavigate the world, he requested that each ship in his expedition carry 18 hourglasses.

Magellan's plan was for some of the hourglasses to run for 30 minutes, some to run for one hour, some to run for two hours and some to run for four hours. All of the hourglasses were the same size, but each had different amounts of sand to measure the time.

Imagine that the hourglasses were made by making two empty cones out of glass and connecting them point to point. In order for the sand to flow correctly, the sand needed to come up to a height of at least 2-inches, but not more than $^3/_4$ the length of the cone. What is the minimum height of each of the cones?

E. 3 inches **G. $5^1/_3$ inches**

F. $4^1/_2$ inches **H. 7 inches**

NEED A CLUE? Imagine putting some arbitrary amount of sand in one cone. We can say that the height that the sand reaches is H, and the volume of the sand as V. Now picture adding sand so that the height of the sand is doubled to 2H, resulting in a volume that can be expressed as 2^3V or 8V.

Reminder: The formula for the volume of a cone (V) is:

$$V = {}^1/_3\pi r^2 h$$

The answer is: G, $5^1/_3$ inches

This ratio is always true: If the height of the sand is 2H, the volume is 8V.

- In our problem, the volume of sand needed to measure four hours is eight times the volume needed for $^1/_2$ hour.
- If the volume increases by a factor of 8, then the height must increase by a factor of 2.
- The maximum height of the sand is twice the minimum height. The problem tells us that the minimum height of sand is 2", so the maximum height of sand must be 4".
- According to the specifications in the problem, the maximum height of sand must be $^3/_4$ the height of the cone. So, $4 \div {}^3/_4 = {}^{16}/_3 = 5^1/_3$"

Recreation and Sports Answers

43. Steve, Steve, Steve, Mary and Steve

Five friends, Steve, Steve, Steve, Mary and Steve go to a baseball game. One of them catches a foul ball. What are the odds that it was a Steve?

A. 5 to 1 in favor **C. <u>4 to 1 in favor</u>** ☜

B. 1 to 5 in favor **D. 1 to 4 in favor**

The answer is C, 4 to 1

There are five friends, and four are named Steve, so the probability of a Steve catching the ball is $^4/_5$ or 80%. However, the question asked for the odds. The fraction $^4/_5$ tells us that out of five catches, a Steve is expected to catch the ball four times and, therefore, not catch the ball one time. In other words, the odds of a ball being caught by a Steve is four for every one ball not caught by a Steve. That's odds of 4 to 1 in favor of a Steve.

44. Team Player

Daniel plays soccer on a team in the local BES ("Busy Every Saturday") soccer league. There are 10 players on his team. At any one time, eight players are on the field. The coach always chooses his players randomly. What percent of the time does Daniel not play?

The answer is: 20%.

An easy way to calculate this is to note that, all things being equal, two of the 10 players will be sitting out at any given time, so everyone will sit $^{2}/_{10}$ (or 20%) of the time.

Another way to solve this problem is to figure out how many different combinations of players can be fielded—and then determine how many include Daniel.

Choosing at random, there are 10 players that the coach can pick for the first person to sit out, and nine choices remaining for the second person to sit out. That would be 90 choices for players to sit out. However, it doesn't matter whether a player is picked first or second to sit out. To take that into account, we need to divide by the number of ways two players can be chosen (2). Therefore, we get $^{90}/_{2} = 45$ possible ways for two players to sit on the bench.

Next, we need to figure out how many of those ways include Daniel. There are nine combinations of Daniel and one other player sitting out. So out of 45 possible choices, 9 include Daniel. $^{9}/_{45}$ reduces to $^{1}/_{5}$, or 20%.

45. Round Robin

In a soccer league, there are 10 teams. They play in a round-robin tournament, where each team plays each of the other teams. Each time a team wins, it gets three points. For each tie, the team gets one point. For a loss, the team gets zero points.

After six weeks of play, the top four teams are the Cantaloupes, the Zebras, the Armadillos and the Beavers. Their standings are:

Rank	Team	Points
1	Cantaloupes	21
2	Zebras	17
3	Armadillos	15
4	Beavers	14

Assume the Cantaloupes don't lose any of their last three games. They only win or tie. Is it possible for the Beavers to win with the most points?

The answer is: No

Because the Cantaloupes don't lose any games, we know they will have at least 24 points at the end of the tournament. The Beavers have 10 points fewer than 24 to start with, and the most points they can earn, if they win all three remaining games, is nine. Therefore, the Beavers can't win—but they could come in second.

46. Batting Average

Joe Slugger is on the Mudville Nine baseball team. With 200 times at bat, Joe has a batting average of .250. Batting average is equal to the number of hits divided by the total number of times at bat. Of his next 100 times at bat, how many hits does Joe need to bring his batting average up to .300?

The answer is: 40

To have a batting average of .300 after 300 times at bat, one needs to have 300 x .300 = 90 hits.

Joe has a batting average of .250 after 200 times at bat. That means that Joe has had 200 x 0.25 = 50 hits. Therefore, to ensure a batting average of .300, Joe needs 90 – 50 = 40 hits out of the next 100 times at bat.

47. Play Ball!

Ryan and Jeremy finished playing their first two baseball games of the season. Their statistics for these games were:

	Ryan		Jeremy	
	Hits/ At Bat	Batting Average	Hits/ At Bat	Batting Average
Game 1	3 for 7	.429	1 for 2	.500
Game 2	1 for 4	.250	2 for 7	.286

Who has a higher batting average for the season?

The answer is: Ryan

For the two games, Jeremy has batted 3 for 9, which is a batting average of .333. Meanwhile, Ryan has batted 4 for 11, which is a batting average of a little bit more than .333 (4 for 12 would be .333); 4 for 11 is .364. So, even though Jeremy has a higher average in each game, Ryan has a better batting average over all.

Averaging averages just doesn't work. Instead, add up all the parts, and find the overall average.

48. Cracking the Lock

Lance rode his bike to the store. He wanted to keep it safe, so he brought along his bike lock. It had a combination lock with four wheels on it, and each wheel has the numbers 0 through 9. If you put the wheels in the correct order, the lock opens.

Now, Lance has a bad memory, so to help him remember the combination he used only even numbers 2, 4, 6 and 8, without duplication. Lance also put them in random order. Of course, Lance has forgotten the combination. What are the most combinations Lance will have to try to open the lock?

The answer is: 24

You could do this by making a list of all the combinations, but let's try something faster.

If Lance starts by setting the first wheel, he has four numbers to choose among: 2, 4, 6 or 8. After he picks one of those numbers, he can't use it again. So, for the second wheel, he has only three numbers from which to choose. Similarly, for the third wheel, there would be only two numbers from which to choose. Then, for the last wheel, he would have only one number left. So, to figure out how many different choices Lance has, multiply the number of choices for the 1st wheel (4) by the number of choices for the 2nd wheel (3) etc. until he runs out of wheels.

In this case, it would be 4 x 3 x 2 x 1 = 24 choices

As you might expect, this kind of thing comes up a lot, so they gave a special name to it. It is called a permutation, defined as "an ordered list without repetition." The calculation we used to find this permutation also has a special name. It is called a factorial. The factorial of a whole number n is the product of all positive integers less than or equal to n. This is written as n!. For example 4! = 4 x 3 x 2 x 1 = 24. The first six factorials are useful to remember: 1! = 1, 2! = 2, 3! = 6, 4! = 24, 5! = 120 and 6! = 720.

49. Slam Dunk

Sixty-four basketball teams have reached the playoffs. Each team plays until it loses. Teams continue to play until only one team remains. What's the fewest number of games that need to be played to determine the winner?

The answer is 63.

63 is also the greatest number of games. Consider the classic playoff set-up, where there are 32 games for the 64 teams in the first round:

There are 16 games among the remaining 32 teams, followed by 8, 4, 2 and 1 game. $1 + 2 + 4 + 8 + 16 + 32 = 63$. It is interesting to note that all the numbers involved are a power of 2. Notice: $2^0 + 2^1 + 2^2 + 2^3 + 2^4 + 2^5 = 2^6 - 1 = 63$.

If you think about it, there will be one remaining team only when the other 63 have lost one game. Since every game has one winner and one loser, it takes exactly 63 games to produce 63 losers—and one winning team.

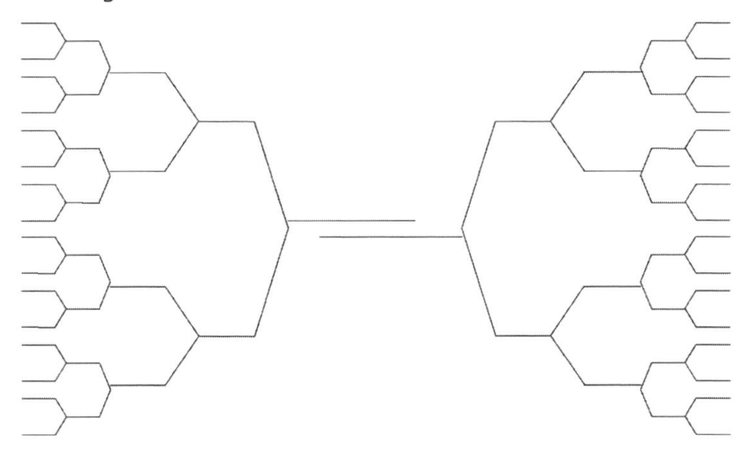

50. Super Sprinter

World-class sprinter Allyson Fleetfeet can run the 100-meter dash in about 10 seconds. If Allyson could maintain that pace for an entire marathon (26 miles and 385 yards), about how long would it her take to finish?

A. around 10 minutes
B. around 1 hour
C. around 3 hours
D. around 6 hours

The answer is: B, around 1 hour

- First, convert Allyson's speed to kilometers per second: 100m/10sec x 1km/1000m = 0.01 km/s.
- To estimate the length of the marathon in kilometers, we toss out the 385 yards and get the equation 26mi x 1km/.6mi = 26 x 1/0.6 km.
- Now the problem becomes "What is $^1/_{0.6}$?" Well, $^1/_{0.5}$ is 2 and $^1/_{0.67}$ is 1.5 so $^1/_{0.6}$ must be somewhere in between.
- Using what we know, we find that $^{26}/_{0.5}$ = 52 and $^{26}/_{0.67}$ = 39. We know the answer is in the middle there somewhere, so let's pick 45 km (because it is easy to work with).
- To get the time it will take to run the marathon, we need to divide the distance by the rate in the units (km/s). The formula is 45km/(0.01km/s), or 45km/(0.01km/s)= 4500 seconds.
- We can convert 4,500 seconds to hours by dividing by 3,600 (60 minutes x 60 seconds = 3,600 seconds in an hour).
- The answer is $^{4,500}/_{3,600}$ = $^5/_4$ = 1.25 hours

As it turns out, it's impossible to sprint for that long. World-class marathoners take between 2 and 2.25 hours to finish a race.

51. Perfect Scores

Match the perfect score with the sport:

A) 300	**1) Cross country**
B) 180	**2) Bowling**
C) 15	**3) Baseball**
D) Shut out	**4) Darts**

The answer is: C(1), A(2), D(3), B(4)

Bowling consists of 10 frames, during which the bowler gets two chances to knock down 10 bowling pins. If the bowler knocks down all the pins with one ball (a strike), the score for the frame will be 10 plus the number of pins knocked down by the next two balls. If the bowler knocks down all the pins with both balls (a spare), the score for the frame is 10 plus the number of pins knocked down with the next ball. Otherwise, the score is the number of pins knocked down. The most that can be scored in one frame is 30 (three consecutive strikes), and this is true for every frame, including the 10th (if you get a strike in the 10th, you get two extra balls). 30 x 10 = 300, the perfect bowling score.

Darts: The standard dartboard is divided into 20 numbered sections, scoring from one to 20 points. Within the numbered sections, there are also double scoring areas and triple scoring areas. And the circular area in the center of the board is the bullseye. Each player gets three darts to throw in one turn. The highest score possible with three darts is 180, when all three darts land in the triple 20. Here's how to keep score:

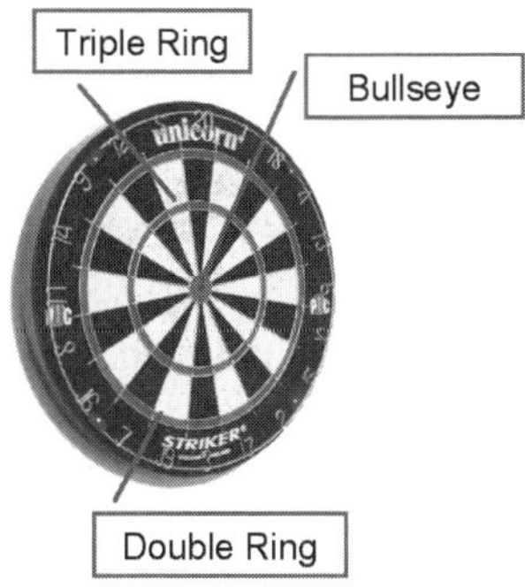

- Hitting one of the large portions of each of the numbered sections, scores precisely the points value of that section.
- Hitting the thin outer portions of these sections, scores double the points value of that section.
- Hitting the thin inner portions of these sections, roughly halfway between the outer boundry and the central circle, scores triple the points value of that section.

• The central circle is divided into an outer ring worth 25 and an inner circle, the bullseye, worth 50 points.

In cross country, scores are usually awarded based on how each team's top five runners finished in the race. For a team to get a perfect score of 15 (1 + 2 + 3 + 4 + 5), their runners must finish in each of the top five positions.

Baseball is different than the other games listed. In baseball, a "perfect score" is for one team to prevent the other team from scoring any points, called runs. So, the final score of the game would be something to zero (i.e. 1-0, 3-0, 32-0, etc.), When one team prevents the other from scoring any runs, it is called a "shut out". A "no hitter" occurs when the opposing team doesn't get any hits, although it is possible for that team to score runs without the benefit of a hit. A "perfect game" is very, very rare. When a baseball pitcher throws a perfect game, the pitcher does not allow anyone from the opposing team to reach first base. 27 batters up, 27 batters out. This means no walks, no errors, no hits and especially no home runs!

52. Tennis, Anyone?

The serve of a professional tennis player can travel between 120 mph and 150 mph. Sally is just learning to play, so her serve travels at only about 80 mph (120 feet per second). A serve that can't be returned is called an ace. Typically, an ace will travel about 80 feet to land right in the corner of the court. If Sally hits the tennis ball on her serve when it is seven feet off the ground, what would be the best trajectory for her to try to achieve?

A. A positive slope (ascending)
B. A slope of zero (moving horizontally)
C. A negative slope (descending)

The answer is: A, a positive slope (ascending)

If the tennis ball gets hit horizontally and has to go about 80 feet traveling at 120 feet per second, then it takes 80ft/120ft/s, or $^2/_3$ (0.67) seconds to go that distance horizontally.

Here's how to figure out how long it will take for an object to fall. A good approximation for how long it takes for something to fall is this equation: $t = {}^1/_4 \sqrt{h}$, where t is in seconds and h is in feet. So if the tennis ball were dropped from seven feet, it would take $^1/_4 \sqrt{7}$ seconds. In this case, it's easiest to use a calculator to find the square root of 7, which is about 2.65. Multiply by $^1/_4$, and you'll find that the fall takes about 0.66 seconds.

So gravity will pull the ball to the ground just before it goes the required distance. In order to get the ball to hit the ground at the appropriate distance, it must be hit at a slight incline. That means it must have a positive, or ascending, slope.

53. Triple Doubles

In Monopoly, you roll two dice and move the number of spaces equal to the sum of the dice. If you roll doubles, you get to roll again. However, if you roll 3 doubles in a row, you go directly to jail, do not pass Go and do not collect $200. What are the chances of this happening?

A. 1 in 6
B. 1 in 36
C. 1 in 216
D. 1 in a million

NEED A CLUE? First, determine the chances of rolling doubles on the first roll.

The answer is: C, 1 in 216

There are six outcomes possible for each die, making a total of 36 possible outcomes. There are six ways to roll doubles (1-1, 2-2, 3-3, 4-4, 5-5, and 6-6). Six in 36 is the same as $^1/_6$. The same holds true on the second and third rolls. Since the rolls don't influence each other (the dice have no recollection of what was rolled each time), we need to multiply the results of each separate roll together. When we do, we get: $^1/_6 \times {^1/_6} \times {^1/_6} = {^1/_{216}}$, or 1 in 216.

Economics Answers

54. Scrimp and Save

Right or Wrong: Your dad has agreed to help you save for a baseball bat. The bat costs $100. Your dad has offered to add 10% to whatever you save. You work hard and earn $90. Now, with your dad's contribution, you have enough money for the bat.

The answer is: Wrong!

Dad has agreed to add 10% to the money you actually save. If you saved $90, Dad would add 10%, or $9. That would make your total $90+$9 = $99. One dollar short!

The question, then, is: What amount, plus 10 percent, equals $100?

If S is the amount you plan to save, then this is how the equation looks:

$$S + 0.10 \times S = \$100$$

Simplify that to:

$$S\,(1+0.1) = \$100 \qquad S = \frac{\$100}{1.1} \qquad S = \$90.91$$

So, the amount of money you have to save is $90.91. Now, when your dad adds 10% of that value (rounded off to the nearest penny), he puts in $9.09 and voila, you have the money you need!

> **Hmm!** This equation is essentially the same as the basic equation used to calculate simple bank interest.
> The equation is P (1 + i) = B, where P is the principal, i is the interest, and B is the balance. (See question 65.)

55. A Good Investment

As an employee of Dim Bulb Industries, you have an opportunity to invest some of your hard-earned money into one of their investment plans. The way their plan works is that every five years, the Dim Bulb financial advisors select three investments from which you can pick. Your return on the investment is governed by an equation that is a function of what year (Y) of the five-year cycle it is. Here are equations for the growth of the investments. Which choice provides the best rate of return?

> **A. Linear Growth: 35^Y**
> **B. Cubic Growth: Y^3**
> **C. Exponential Growth: 2^Y**

The answer is: A, linear growth

On the graph, we can see that at six years, the cubic growth curve crosses over the linear curve and quickly becomes the better investment. If we extend the time line out to 11 years, we can see that the exponential curve crosses the cubic curve at 10 years. So If Dim Bulb let the investments run longer then one of the other curves would be better, but with only a relatively short cycle of five years, the linear growth is the best.

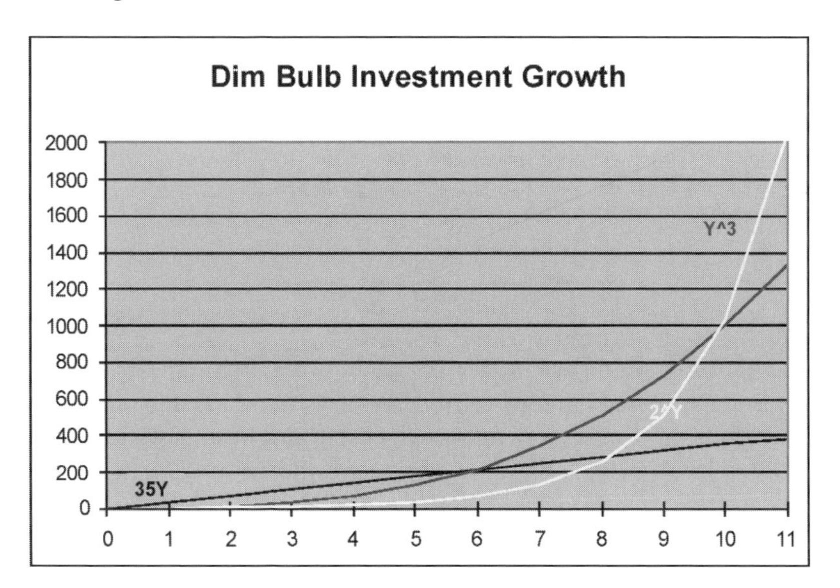

56. Realty Check

Three realtors open an office together. After some length of time they each put up a poster showing their success at selling houses. All three charts represent accurate data over the same time period. If you were going to sell your house and use one of the three realtors, based on their sales chart, which one do you think would be the best pick?

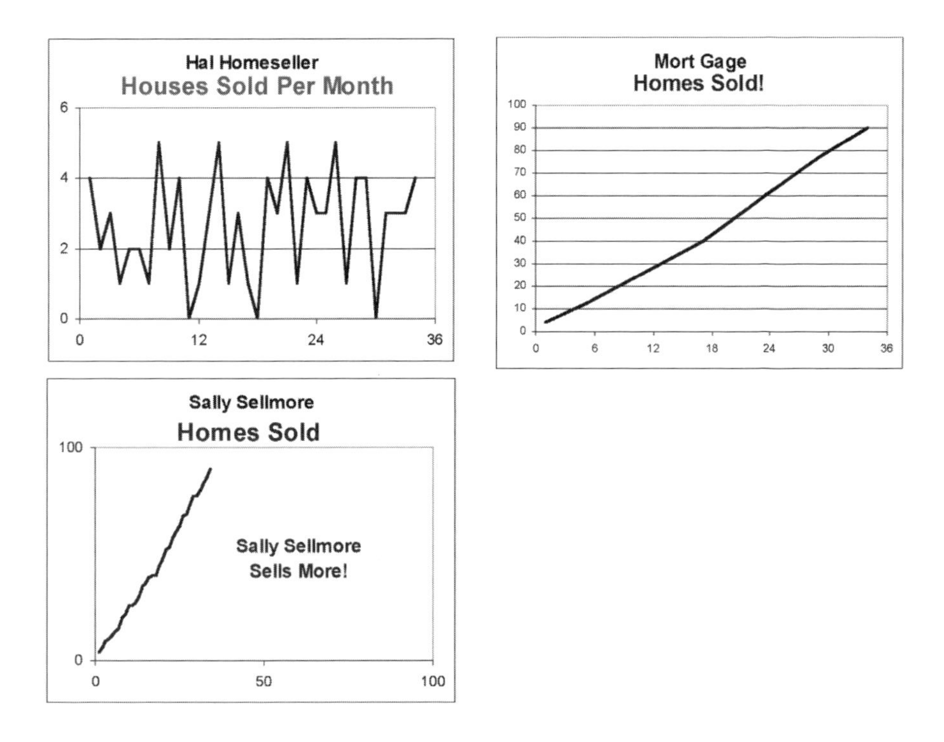

The answer is: They have all sold exactly the same.

The data displayed looks misleading because they are meant to. This is one of the most real-life things in this book. Data can be manipulated and represented a number of different ways. It is because of this that everyone needs a basic understanding of how to distinguish data truth from downright data lies.

Hal Homeseller has done the worst job at creating a marketing tool. His data, although correct, are difficult to evaluate, especially compared with the other two charts. Hal shows his data as homes sold per month. Some months he has sold five houses and in some months he has sold no houses at all. Does he really want his potential customers to see that stated so obviously?

Sally and Mort show almost identical curves. Sally's shows some fluctuations to make it seem a little more real than Mort's. Because Sally has put her curve on a longer time scale (the x-axis), it makes her success appear to take place over a shorter period of time than Mort's. Also, because Sally only has the value of 100 on her chart you tend to think that she has sold about 100 houses. Mort, on the other hand, has several numbers on his chart, so you will tend to remember that he sold about 90 homes. The reality is that they sold the same number.

Remember, data can be represented a number of different ways. If the way they are shown to you is confusing, ask to see the data displayed differently, or ask to see the raw data and do your own analysis. The way data are presented falls under the field of statistics. Remember this adage: "There are lies, big lies, and statistics."

57. Examining eCommerce

Julio has been saving up all year to buy the newest video game system, PONG 8000. Being a good consumer, Julio has done his research on pricing before he gives up his hard-earned money. In the end, there are three stores where he is considering making his purchase. Ohms Emporium is a local store while OverWhelmed.com and We Sell the World are online businesses. Based on the following table, which is the best deal?

Store	Price	Discount	Tax	Shipping & Handling	Delivery Time
Ohms Emporium	$ 260	-	10%	-	pick up
Over Whelmed.com	$ 255	-	-	$ 25.00	5-7 days
We Sell the World	$ 250	5% (online only)	10%	$ 20.00	2-3 days

The answer is: OverWhelmed.com

Even though We Sell the World has the lowest price and a discount, the tax and shipping charges bring your final cost up:

$250 (100% – 5%) (100 + 10%) + $20 = $250(.95)(1.1) + $20 = $281.25.

- The total price from Ohms Emporium is $260 (100% + 10%) = $260 (1.1) = $286.
- The total price from OverWhelmed.com is $255 + $25 = $280

Julio will have to wait a little longer, but he'll save money if he orders from OverWhelmed.com.

58. Chuck the Woodchuck

Giles notices an advertisement in the newspaper for an in-store discount of 50% off Woodchuck Chuckin' Wood. This is good news for Giles, who knows precisely how much wood his woodchuck Chuck chucks, since his woodchuck can chuck wood. At the store, Giles notes that Chuck's favorite flavor of Chuckin' Wood (maple, of course) has a coupon for an additional 50% off the lowest marked price. The cashier says that 50% + 50% = 100%, so the bag is free. Is the cashier correct?

The answer is: No

Giles, being exceptionally honest, corrects the cashier and explains that he should not get the Chuckin' Wood for free. He should get 75% off.

Here's why:

- The first discount is 50%, so the price becomes 50% of the original price.
- The second discount is against the discounted price or 50% of 50%, or 25% of the original price.
- So, the total discount of the original price is 50% + 25% = 75%.

59. DVD Deals

Ebony goes shopping for a new DVD. Luckily for her, the Dandy Dave's DVD Shoppe is having a sale. Buy one DVD and get 20% off, buy two and each DVD is 30% off, buy three or more and each DVD is 40% off. Ebony sees five DVDs she likes, but realizes she only has a $25 gift card to buy the DVDs. When making her selections, Ebony must remember the 5% tax and the $1.50 fee that will be taken from her gift card each time she uses it. Using the table, find the most DVDs Ebony can purchase while keeping within her $25 budget.

Movie Title	Price
Rabbit Fire	$15
Ro.Go.Pa.G.	$15
Le Notti Bianche	$20
The Crowd	$20
Day of Wrath (The Director's Cut)	$25

The answer is: 2

Obviously, the best thing would be to be able to take advantage of the 40% off discount. So, Ebony picks the three least expensive DVDs. Together they cost $15 + $15 + $20 = $50. If that is discounted by 40% then the cost goes down to $30. Calculating what 40% of a number is might seem difficult, so let's think about it differently. Figuring out 10 percent of a number is easy; you just divide by 10. So 10% of $50 is $5. 40% of a number is four times 10% of that number, so 40% of $50 is 4 x $5, which equals $20. Therefore, the discounted price is $50 – $20 = $30. But, having done that calculation, we notice that $30 is larger than $25. So, now we look to the 30% discount on two items.

We can do similar calculations on the two least expensive DVDs and find that they equal $30, minus $9 ($30 x 0.3) for a discounted price of $21. This is under $25. But wait, there are two more things we need to consider.

The first is tax. There is a sales tax of 5% that we have to add on. To figure out what the tax is we can recognize that 5% is half of 10%. 10% is $2.10, and half of that is $1.05. We add that to $21 and get $22.05.

The second thing we have to do is add on the $1.50 service fee to get $23.55, which is less than $25. Therefore, Ebony can buy, at most, two DVDs.

60. Peanut Whiz Kid

In Gooberville, grocery stores are required to list on the shelves not only the price per item, but also a unit price. The unit price helps the buyer figure out quickly which package of a certain product is the better deal.

One day Ellerína goes to SavClub to buy Peanut Whizzes. Next to each other on the shelf, she sees the Gooberville Greats brand that goes with the first label.

Next to it, she finds the Groovy Gill's brand with this label:

Which brand is the better price?

NEED A CLUE? Look for a mistake that was made on one of the unit price labels.

The answer is: Groovy Gill's

While the Gooberville Greats brand uses price per ounce as its basic unit of measure, Groovy Gill's is basing its unit price on the price of a dozen boxes, not price per ounce. In this case, we have to go back to the old fashioned way of doing math, in our heads.

The first thing to notice is that the Gooberville Greats package is 32 ounces—twice the weight of the Groovy Gill's package. That being the case, if the Gooberville Greats price is less than twice the price of Groovy Gill's, then it is the better price. $4.37 \div 2.07$ is greater than 2, so the better deal is Groovy Gill's.

61. We All Scream for Ice Cream

Ogg and Nahtogg go to RocksCo to pick up a 55-gallon drum of their favorite ice cream (Rocky Road, of course). They plan on opening an ice cream shop, where they will sell 4-oz. scoops of ice cream for 50¢ each. They pay $220 for the ice cream and nothing for the ice cream cones (because they won't be invented for another 10,000 years, at the 1904 St. Louis World's Fair). If they sell all their ice cream, how much profit will they make?

A. They will lose money **C. $660** ☜
B. $180 **D. $1100**

The answer is: C, $660

First, let's figure out the cost per gallon of the ice cream. The cost of one gallon of ice cream is $220 ÷ 55 = $4.

Now, let's figure out the profit Ogg and Nahtogg will make per gallon:

- 1 gallon = 4 quarts = 8 pints = 16 cups = 128 oz.
- Since each scoop is 4 oz., each gallon would yield 128 ÷ 4 = 32 scoops.
- At 50¢ per scoop, they will receive $16 per gallon.
- Profit equals revenue (how much money they make) minus cost (what they pay to get what they sell), or $16 - $4 = $12 profit per gallon, and 55 x $12 = $660 per 55 gallon drum.

62. Here's a Tip

In Gooberville, there is a tax of 7% on food sold in a restaurant. It is also customary to give a gratuity (also called a tip) to show your appreciation for the service. Typically, a good tip is between 15% and 20% of the total before the tax is added.

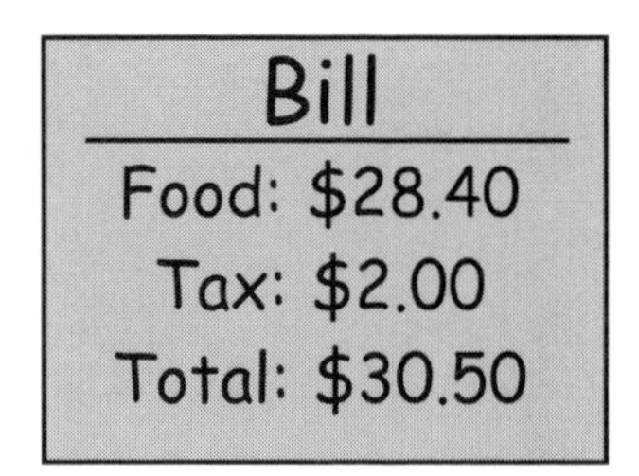

Buffy goes to a restaurant. Her bill comes to $28.50, and the tax comes to $2.00. Estimate a tip between 15% and 20%.

☞ **A. $4.50--$5.00** **C. $10**
B. $6.00–$7.50 **D. None of the above**

The answer is: A, $4.50–$5.00

Any tip between $4.28 and $5.70 would work. There are many ways to estimate a tip. Here are some good ones:

Method 1:

- The tax is 7% and the bill shows us that value is $2. If we double the tax, we know that 14% is $4.
- If we triple the tax we find that 21% is $6.
- 14% is too low and 21% is too high, so we can split the difference (which is another way to say find the average) and get $5. That's a 17.5% tip.

Method 2:

- If you move the decimal point to the left one place, you get 10% of the bill. Now you can add half of that number for a 15% tip, or double it if the waiter did a really good job!

63. Buying Tires

Farmer Kabibble needs to get new tires for his truck. At the tire store, he finds that there are two different-sized tires that would work. The Super Deluxe Dirt Grabbers are 60 cm in diameter, and the Premium Road Grippers are 50 cm in diameter. The price of the Premium Road Grippers is 10% less than the price of the Super Deluxe Dirt Grabbers. Which tires are the better deal?

The answer is: The Super Deluxe Dirt Grabbers (the more expensive ones).

For a given number of miles, tires with a smaller diameter will suffer more wear than tires with a larger diameter. This is because the wear of a tire is related to how many times the tire goes around on the ground. Tires with smaller diameters need to go around more times to cover the same distance as larger diameter tires. This is because the circumference (C) of a circle is directly proportional to its diameter (d). The formula is $C = \pi d$ (remember that π is approximately 3.14).

The less expensive tires have a circumference that is 5/6 that of the more expensive tires. The price of the less expensive tires is 9/10 the price of the other tires. The bottom line is that if you purchase the Premium Road Grippers you save 10% on the price but get 16% fewer miles before the tires wear out.

So, the more expensive tires are actually the better deal.

64. Calling Card

Mary has a telephone calling card. The first minute costs $1.00 and all subsequent minutes or fractions of minutes cost 10¢. At the motel where Mary is staying, it costs $5 per day to make all the local calls she wants. Mary plans to stay one day and make three local calls that will last 8 to 10 minutes each. Should she use the local phone service or her calling card?

The answer is: Local Phone Service

With the calling card, three eight-minute calls would cost $1.70 per call ($1.00 for the first minute, plus $0.10 x 7, or $0.70, for the next 7 minutes.) That would cost 3 x $1.70 = $5.10 for three calls.

If each call is 10 minutes, then a call will cost $1.90 ($1.00 + 9 x $0.10), and three would cost 3 x $1.90 = $5.70.

Either way, the local phone service (at $5 per day) is the better deal.

65. Interesting Interest

You have $100 in a bank account earning 2% interest per year compounded annually. If the interest rate never changes and you never add any more to the account, about how long will it take until you have $200 in your account?

A. 5 years **C. 36 years**
B. 16 years **D. 50 years**

The answer is C, 36 years.

Interest is money the bank pays you for putting your money in the bank. The bank puts money in your account based on how much money is already in your account. So 2% interest on $100 means that the bank will give you $2 for the year. That's 2% of your money. Now, compound interest is interest that is added to the original principal ("principal" is a term for the money with which you started). New interest is then calculated, not only on the principal, but also on the interest that has been added. The more frequently interest is compounded, the faster the principal grows.

At this point there are two ways to proceed. We can estimate the answer or go for mathematical precision. Let's try estimating first. In the world of finance, there is a standard estimation used called the "Rule of 72." The rule states that the number of years it takes for a bank account to double can be estimated by dividing 72 by the interest rate (ignoring the percent). In this case, we would divide 72 by 2 (representing 2%), and the result is 36 years.

Now, for all you sticklers for precision: To calculate bank interest, use the equation $P(1 + i)^n = B$, where P is the principal, i is the annual interest rate, n is the number of years, and B is the balance. So, if you have $100 in a bank account that pays 2% interest compounded annually then at the end of the first year you will have $100 (1 + 0.02) = $102. Assuming you don't add any money, at the end of the second year you will have $102; apply the compounded interest to that amount, $102 (1+.02) = $104.04, and you have your new balance.

So, we either have to do the above calculation until the result is at least $200 or we need to solve the following equation for n: $100(1+.02)^n = 200$. Yikes! What do you say we go back to the estimation and the Rule of 72?

66. Gaging a Mortgage

Consuela has decided to buy the purple house at 1999 Alphabet Street. Her realtor at Prince Properties, Nelson Rogers, has negotiated a purchase price of $200,000. After her down payment, she will need to borrow $167,000 from the Bank of Gooberville. This is a 30-year fixed rate mortgage with monthly payments and an annual interest rate of 6% (in this case, interest is the money she pays the bank for the use of the money).

Each month, Consuela will pay the bank $1,000. A portion of each payment is used to pay the interest she owes the bank, and the remaining money goes to reduce the loan balance. This is called "amortizing the loan." At the end of 360 months (30 years), the last payment will reduce the loan balance to zero, and Consuela will own the house outright. About how much interest will Consuela end up paying over the life of the loan?

A. $ 10,000 C. $100,000

B. $ 50,000 D. $200,000 ☜

NEED A CLUE? The easiest way to think about this is to calculate how much Consuela will pay total, and then subtract the portion that repays the principal. The principal is the amount of money that she owes the bank at any given moment.

The answer is: D, $200,000

Here is how to estimate the amount of interest. Begin with the basic facts about Consuela's monthly payments:

- 360 months x $1,000 per month = $360,000 total.
- $360,000 - $167,000 = $193,000, which is very close to $200,000.

Compare the amortization schedule for the first 12 months with the last 12 months:

First 12 Months				
Month	Payment	Interest	Principal Repayment	Remaining Balance
				$167,000.00
1	$1,000.00	$833.38	$166.62	$166,833.38
2	$1,000.00	$832.55	$167.45	$166,665.93
3	$1,000.00	$831.71	$168.29	$166,497.64
4	$1,000.00	$830.87	$169.13	$166,328.52
5	$1,000.00	$830.03	$169.97	$166,158.54
6	$1,000.00	$829.18	$170.82	$165,987.73
7	$1,000.00	$828.33	$171.67	$165,816.05
8	$1,000.00	$827.47	$172.53	$165,643.53
9	$1,000.00	$826.61	$173.39	$165,470.14
10	$1,000.00	$825.75	$174.25	$165,295.88
11	$1,000.00	$824.88	$175.12	$165,120.76
12	$1,000.00	$824.00	$176.00	$164,944.76

Last 12 Months				
Month	Payment	Interest	Principal Repayment	Remaining Balance
349	$1,000.00	$57.99	$942.01	$10,677.64
350	$1,000.00	$53.28	$946.72	$9,730.92
351	$1,000.00	$48.56	$951.44	$8,779.48
352	$1,000.00	$43.81	$956.19	$7,823.30
353	$1,000.00	$39.04	$960.96	$6,862.34
354	$1,000.00	$34.25	$965.75	$5,896.58
355	$1,000.00	$29.43	$970.57	$4,926.01
356	$1,000.00	$24.58	$975.42	$3,950.59
357	$1,000.00	$19.71	$980.29	$2,970.31
358	$1,000.00	$14.82	$985.18	$1,985.13
359	$1,000.00	$9.91	$990.09	$995.03
360	$1,000.00	$4.97	$995.03	$0.00

In the early months, more than 80% of each payment goes to the bank to pay interest due, and the loan balance slowly decreases. In the last few months, the situation reverses as very little of each payment is required to pay any interest since the loan balance is so small.

In the real world, the payment amount is determined by the interest rate (i), the loan balance (L), and the number of payments (n). It is generally calculated using a calculator, spreadsheet, or computer program. But just in case you find yourself with time on your hands, you can find the payment P with this formula: $P = (^{i}/_{12}) \times L / (1-[1/(1+^{i}/_{12})]^{n})$

That explains the need for electronic assistance!

Disclaimer: If you used a financial calculator, you would find the monthly payment would be closer to $1001.25. Congratulations if you caught this!

67. Where Credit is Due

Ogg has just received his first MasterRock credit card ("Don't leave your cave without it!"). In the first month, Ogg charges way more money than he can afford. His charges equal $1,000, mostly iRock downloads. MasterRock tells him that he needs to make a minimum payment of 2% of the balance each month, but no less than $10.00. However, for every month after the 1st month, he will have interest added to his bill in the amount of 1.5% of the outstanding balance. Ogg decides not to charge any more until he pays off the entire bill. Assuming Ogg pays only the minimum each month, about how long will it take Ogg to off his balance?

A. 1 year C. 10 years

B. 5 years D. 20 years ☞

The answer is: D, 20 years

It will take almost 20 years to pay off the balance making minimum payments. The minimum payment (2% of the balance) is barely enough to pay the interest due on the balance (1.5%). That means very little of the payment will reduce the outstanding balance. This is another example of an amortized payment. Here is what the schedule looks like for the first twelve months:

	Payment	Interest	Applied to Outstanding Balance	Outstanding Balance
				1000.00
1	20.00	0.00	20.00	980.00
2	19.60	14.70	4.90	975.10
3	19.50	14.63	4.87	970.23
4	19.40	14.55	4.85	965.38
5	19.31	14.48	4.83	960.55
6	19.21	14.41	4.80	955.75
7	19.12	14.34	4.78	950.97
8	19.02	14.26	4.76	946.21
9	18.92	14.19	4.73	941.48
10	18.83	14.12	4.71	936.77
11	18.74	14.05	4.69	932.08
12	18.64	13.98	4.66	927.42
Total	230.29	157.71	72.58	

Three things to notice:

1. No interest is due the 1st month, which means that if Ogg had paid off the balance immediately, there would have been no interest due.

2. Since the outstanding balance is declining, the minimum payment due is also declining.

3. After 12 months, almost $^2/_3$ of his payments have gone to interest and only $^1/_3$ has gone to pay down what he owes.

In the 229th month (19 years, 1 month), the outstanding balance drops below $10.00, so Ogg finally pays off the balance. So, in just over 19 years, Ogg will have made $2,871.27 in payments, of which $1,000 repays the original balance, and the remaining $1,871.27 is interest he pays to the credit card company.

The moral of the story is: maximize your credit card payments, and you will reduce interest expenses. Or better yet, never charge more than you can afford, and pay your total balance every month.

The credit card company wants you to buy a lot and make minimum payment because that is how they make their money. The interest rates we mention here are pretty typical. If you make only minimum payments, you can end up paying the credit card company interest almost twice the amount of the original purchase.

68. Goody Goody Gumballs

You are in charge of buying gumballs for the gumball machine. You can either get 850 large gumballs for $50 or 8,500 small gumballs for $100. You can sell the large gumballs for 25¢ each and the small gumballs for 5¢ each. You have $100 to spend. Which type of gumballs should you buy to maximize your profit?

A. The big gumballs **C. It doesn't matter**
B. The small gumballs

The answer is: C, it doesn't matter.

For $100, you can buy 850 x 2 = 1,700 large gumballs, or 8,500 small gumballs. You'll get 1,700 x $0.25 = $425 selling the large gum balls, or 8,500 x $0.05 = $425 selling the small gumballs. The small gumballs are $^1/_5$ the cost, but also make $^1/_5$ the revenue, so it doesn't matter which size gumball you get.

69. Kabibbleberry Jam

Farmer Kabibble is selling jars of Kabibbleberry jam. He guesses that if he set the price at $4.00 that he could sell 120 jars. He thinks that every $1.00 increase means he would sell twenty fewer jars. On the other hand, for every $1.00 decrease, he could sell twenty more jars. If the goal is to maximize his revenue, what price should he charge?

A. $3.00 **C. $5.00**
B. $4.00 **D. $7.00**

The answer is: C, $5.00

Let's set up a chart for all the prices between $0.00 and $10.00:

Price Per Jar	Number of Jars	Total Revenue	Price Per Jar	Number of Jars	Total Revenue
$0.00	200	$0.00	$6.00	80	$480.00
$1.00	180	$180.00	$7.00	60	$420.00
$2.00	160	$320.00	$8.00	40	$320.00
$3.00	140	$420.00	$9.00	20	$180.00
$4.00	120	$480.00	$10.00	0	$0.00
$5.00	100	$500.00			

Or here's how the data look on a line graph:

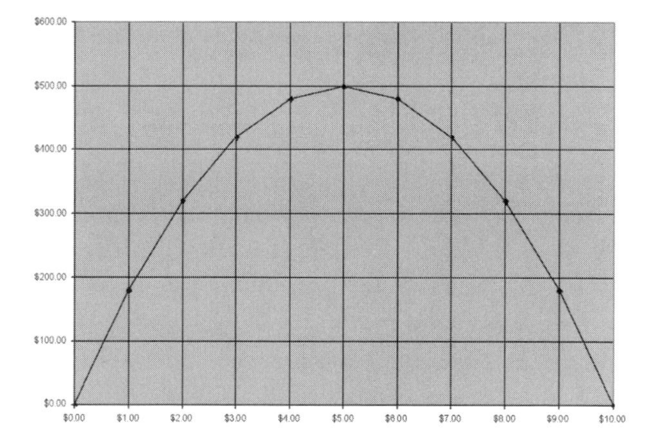

This is a parabola defined by the equation: $y = 20x(10-x)$. The maximum revenue is the highest point, the vertex, of the parabola, which occurs at $5.00 per jar.

Hmm! All sellers have a trade-off to consider when setting prices. If the price is too high, they won't sell very many items, and thus not make a lot of money. But, if the price is too low, they'll sell a lot at a low price, and still not make a lot of money. The price needs to be set to balance the consumers' demand with the producers' supply. If demand goes up, supply goes down, so the price should go up. If demand is low, then supply is high, so dropping the price should stimulate demand. In economics, this is called the Law of Supply and Demand.

Nature, Music and Art Answers

70. Nanoseconds

Rear Admiral Grace Murray Hopper (1906–1992) was a U.S. computer scientist and naval officer. She is famous for her nanoseconds visual aid. People (such as generals and admirals) used to ask her why satellite communication took so long, so she started handing out pieces of wire. The length of each piece of wire was the distance that light travels in one nanosecond.

Knowing that light travels at about 186,000 miles per second, about how long were Admiral Hopper's "nanoseconds"?

A. About one inch **C. About one yard**

☞ **B. About one foot**

The answer is: B, about one foot

To figure out how long Admiral Hopper's nanoseconds are, we have to convert the speed of light from miles per second to feet per nanoseconds.

- To convert miles per second to miles per nanosecond we must multiply by 10^{-9} seconds/nanoseconds, thus getting $186{,}000 \times 10^{-9} = 1.86 \times 10^{-4}$ miles per nanosecond.
- Next, we need to turn miles per nanosecond into feet per nanosecond. So, we have to multiply 1.86×10^{-4} by 5280 ft/mile. This calculation is a bit trickier.
- Let's see what happens if we do some estimation. First we round 1.86×10^{-4} up to 2×10^{-4} and then we round 5280 down to 5000. We then get $0.0002 \times 5000 = 1$ ft/nanosecond.
- As it turns out the real answer is .98 ft/nanosecond.

Hmm! Admiral Hopper is also credited with the expression "debugging". She was working on one of the first computers (which were so big you could walk inside). The computer had big mechanical switches inside and a moth had flown in and got squished. Its body prevented the switch from working properly. When someone asked why the computer wasn't running, Grace Hopper said to wait a moment while they "debugged the computer." By the way, you can find the first computer bug (the moth) in the Smithsonian Institute.

71. The Symmetry of Shapes

Let's say you have an image, and that you can rotate that image around some point. If, as you rotate the image, there are times when the image looks identical (when the rotation angle is less than 360°), the image has rotational symmetry at these times. For example, consider an equilateral triangle. Every time the triangle is rotated 120°, it matches up with the original shape:

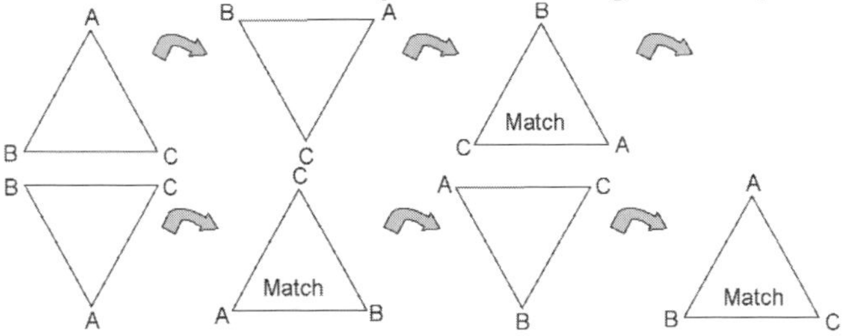

Because the shapes match up three times as the triangle rotates one complete revolution (360°), the triangle is said to have "rotation symmetry order 3".

Shapes in nature can also have rotational symmetry. What is the order of rotational symmetry for each of these objects?

A.

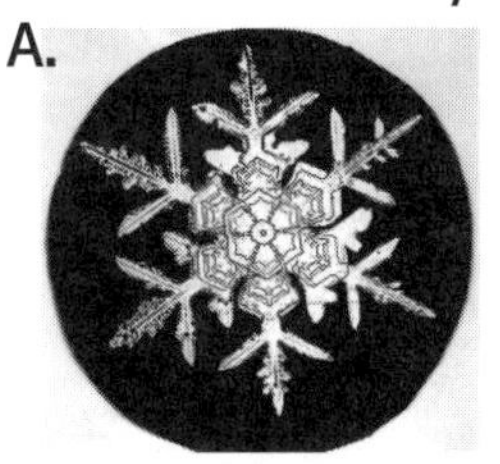

C.

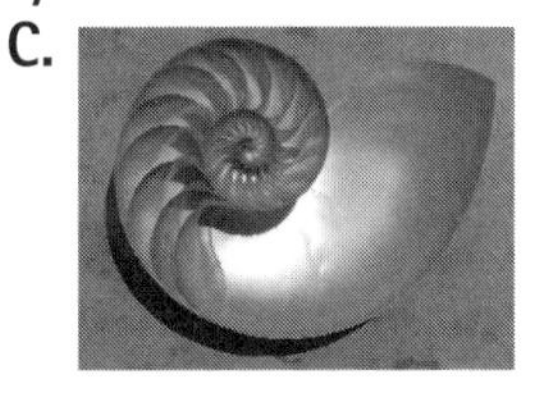

B.

The answer is:

A. The snowflake is an example of an order 6 rotational symmetry.

B. The flower has order 5 symmetry.

C. The nautilus shell does not have rotational symmetry. The shell, however, does represent a shape called a logarithmic spiral.

72. Abby's Birthday

Abby was born on Monday, July 21, 1997. When was the next time her birthday fell on a Monday again?

The answer is: 2003.

There are 365 days in a year and seven days in a week, and 365 divided by7 leaves a remainder of 1. If there were no remainder, then Abby's birthday would be on a Monday every year. Since the remainder is 1, then every year, Abby's birthday is one day later in the week. In 1998, Abby's birthday was on Tuesday, and in 1999, her birthday was on Wednesday. In 2000, it was a leap year, so instead of moving one day later in the week, Abby's birthday moved two days to Friday.

Abby's first 28 years would be like this:

1997 Monday	2004 Wednesday	2011 Thursday	2018 Saturday
1998 Tuesday	2005 Thursday	2012 Saturday	2019 Sunday
1999 Wednesday	2006 Friday	2013 Sunday	2020 Tuesday
2000 Friday	2007 Saturday	2014 Monday	2021 Wednesday
2001 Saturday	2008 Monday	2015 Tuesday	2022 Thursday
2002 Sunday	2009 Tuesday	2016 Thursday	2023 Friday
2003 Monday	2010 Wednesday	2017 Friday	2024 Sunday

Since there are seven days in the week and four years in a leap year cycle, every 28 years the pattern repeats–for now anyway.

It won't work for the year 2100, because years that end in "00" are not leap years, unless the year is also divisible by 400. 2000 was a leap year, and 2400 will be a leap year, but 2100, 2200 and 2300 will not.

73. Scale Model

Michael Angelo has been commissioned to create a bronze sculpture. Before he builds the full-size sculpture, he builds a $^1/_{10}$th-scale solid bronze model. The model weighs two pounds. When the full-sized solid bronze sculpture is finished, will Michael be able to carry it himself?

The answer is: No

The model weighs two pounds and is in $^1/_{10}$th scale. That means each dimension is $^1/_{10}$th its full size. So the volume is decreased by a factor of $(^1/_{10})^3$. In other words, the volume of the model is $^1/_{1000}$ of the full size. Now that we know the model has $^1/_{1000}$ the volume, then we also know that the model, made of the same material as the full version, will be $^1/_{1000}$ the weight.

We know this because weight = density x volume.

The bottom line is that if the model is two pounds, the full size version will weigh 1,000 times the model, or 2,000 pounds. That's way too much for one person to carry.

74. Bubba the Flying Squirrel

The southern flying squirrel has a maximum glide ratio of 3:1. This means that it can glide about three horizontal feet for every vertical foot it falls.

Bubba the flying squirrel climbs to the very top of a 75-foot-tall hickory tree. While nibbling on the hickory nuts, he notices a cute squirrel on a tree 60 feet away and 40 feet below him. In an all-out attempt to impress the cutie, Bubba jumps and glides right to her. What glide ratio did Bubba use?

A. 3:1 **C. 2:1**

☞ **B. 3:2** **D. 4:3**

The answer is: B, 3:2

Glide ratio is the comparison of horizontal distance traveled to vertical distance traveled. Bubba travels 60 feet horizontally and 40 feet vertically, for a glide ratio of 60:40, which reduces to 3:2.

75. Naked Mole Rats

Most queen naked mole rats have average litters of about 11 baby naked mole rats, but some have been known to have 27 babies in a single litter. In a certain hive in sub-Saharan Africa lived a queen naked mole rat that was known to have had around 900 babies over 12 years of being queen. Given what we know, estimate how many litters a year this prolific queen had.

A. 2–4 C. 6–8

☞ B. 4–6 D. 12-16

The answer is: B, 4–6

Since we're estimating, let's try some guesswork:

- Eighty babies a year for 12 years is 960.
- Seventy babies a year would be 840.
- So if we split the difference (find the average), we can estimate about 75 babies a year, on average.
- Now, imagine if each litter had 15 babies (this is an excellent number to pick because it is between 11 and 27 and divides evenly into 75).
- Then that would be five litters a year.

Most queen naked mole rats, though, have only one litter a year.

76. Terrific Tessellation

A tessellation is created when a shape is repeated over and over again covering a plane without any gaps or overlaps. Think of tiles on a floor. Only three regular polygons (shapes that have the same length sides and interior angles) can tessellate a plane. Which of the following cannot?

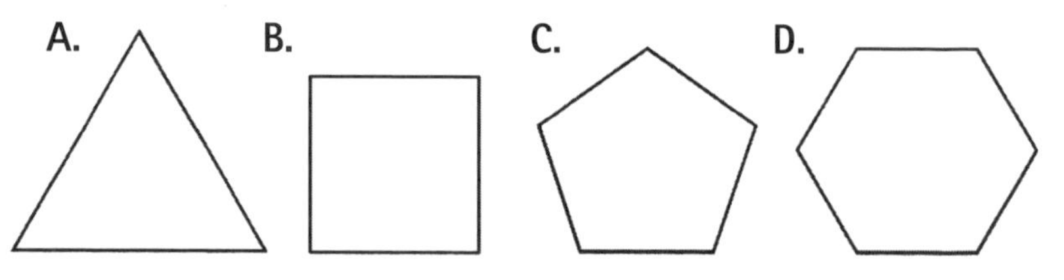

The answer is: C

The other shapes cover the plane without gaps:

a tessellation of triangles

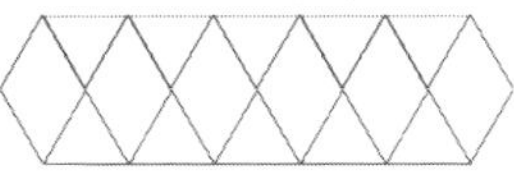

a tessellation of squares

a tessellation of hexagons

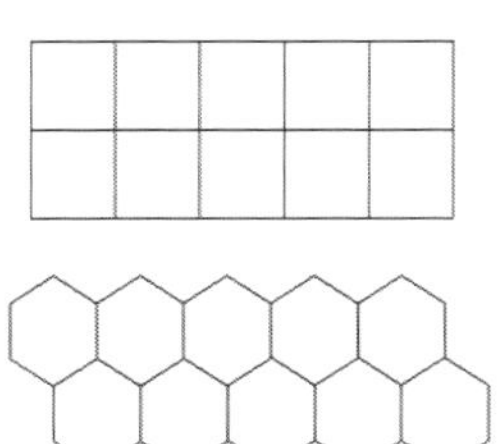

But, no matter how you try, a regular pentagon leaves gaps. The gaps can be fun, though. Try making a five-pointed star in a tessellation of pentagons:

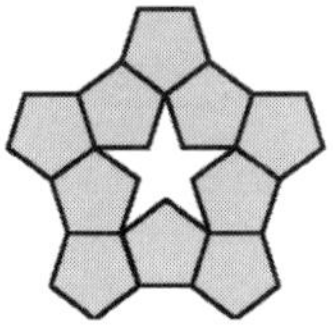

77. Map Quest

You have been challenged to color the map of the United States so that no two adjacent states are colored the same. States that touch at only one corner, such as Utah and New Mexico, are not considered adjacent. What is the fewest number of colors you need to use to win the challenge?

A. 3 **C. 5**

B. 4 **D. 6**

The answer is: B, 4

This result, which is true for any flat (i.e. two-dimensional) map, is known as the Four Color Theorem. In 1852, Francis Guthrie noticed this was true for a map of England and wondered if it was true for other maps. But, for decades, providing a formal proof for the theorem seemed almost impossible.

Finally, in 1976, Kenneth Appel and Wolfgang Haken at the University of Illinois provided a satisfactory proof. What made their solution unique was that this was the first major theorem to be proved using a computer. Unfortunately, the computer's proof is not a set of theorems and equations, so it's not a proof that human beings can verify.

Today, the theorem is generally accepted as proved, but some mathematicians are uncomfortable with the reliance of a computer program to perform human logic.

78. Patching Things Up

Jackie and Rachel need fabric to complete their quilt. Jackie buys a quarter of a yard (9" x 44") of fabric, while Rachel buys a "fat quarter" (18" x 22") of fabric. Both want to cut the fabric efficiently so that they have as many finished $3\,^{1}/_{2}$" x $3\,^{1}/_{2}$" squares as possible. When sewing fabric together, it's important for quilters to leave a $^{1}/_{4}$" seam, so the girls add $^{1}/_{2}$" when they cut their fabric. Who will cut the most squares?

The answer is: Jackie

We figure this out by dividing each dimension of the entire piece of fabric by the dimensions of the 4-inch square. Ignore any remainder.

For Jackie:
9 divided by 4 is 2
44 divided by 4 is 11
The result is 2 x 11 = 22 squares.

For Rachel:
18 divided by 4 is 4
22 divided by 4 is 5
The result is 4 x 5 = 20.

The operation for dividing and taking just the whole number result is called div, and the results could be written 9 div 2 = 4, 44 div 4 = 11, and so on.

79. Tag, You're It

Scientists like to keep track of the number of animals in the wild, especially endangered species. Since actual counting of individual animals is impossible, scientists have developed statistical methods to come up with valid estimates.

One method scientists use to count animal populations is to capture a few animals, identify them with tags and then let them go. Then after a while, they capture a few animals again and see how many have tags.

On one such counting mission, the scientists capture 10 Addax—desert antelopes found in the Sahara—and tag them. Two weeks later they again capture 10 Addax and find that one of them has been tagged. What do the scientists conclude?

A. There are around 20 addax in the wild
☞ B. There are around 100 addax in the wild
C. There are at least 1,000 addax in the wild
D. Addax are easy to catch in the wild

The answer is: B, there are around 100 Addax in the wild

When using this type of count, you must make certain assumptions. In this case, assume that the number of animals caught is a significant number. If you tag 10 pigeons in Trafalgar Square in London, when you catch another 10, the chance of any of them being tagged is very small because there are thousands of pigeons there. On the other hand, Addax are critically endangered, so for them, 10 is likely to be a significant number.

Another assumption is that the animals move around but are still relatively contained in a known region. For instance, it would do little good to tag Canada geese in Canada in the fall and then attempt to recapture them in Canada in winter, after they had started their migration.

Once you meet those criteria, the analysis works this way: when the animals are captured the second time, the percentage of the animals with tags is assumed to represent all the animals with tags. In our case there is one with a tag and that represents 10% of the captured population. So, since originally 10 were tagged, assume that 10% of the total population equals the 10 tagged animals.

So, if 10% of the population is 10 then the population must be equal to 10 ÷ 10% = 10 ÷ 0.1 = 100.

Note: In 2006, National Geographic placed the number of addax in the wild at less than 150.

80. Speed of Sound

Look at the chart, and use interpolation to find the speed of sound at 16,000 feet.

A. 750 mph **C. 718 mph** ☜

B. 720 mph **D. 701 mph**

Altitude	Speed of Sound
0	761
1,000	758
5,000	748
10,000	734
15,000	721
20,000	706
25,000	693
30,000	678
35,000	663

NEED A CLUE? One of the simplest methods of interpolation is linear interpolation (sometimes known as lerp). Generally, linear interpolation takes two data points, say (x_a, y_a) and (x_b, y_b), and the point (x, y), called the interpolant. This is a point in between the other two. Typically x is known and y is solved for. The formula to solve for y is:

$$y = y_a + \frac{(x_b - x_a)(y_b - y_a)}{(x_b - x_a)}$$

The answer is: C, 718 mph

The fast way:

Using test-taking skills, we can find the answer this way. Sixteen-thousand is between 15,000 and 20,000. The speed of sound at 16,000 should be somewhere between 721 (speed of sound at 15,000) and 706 (speed of sound at 20,000), and it should be a little closer to 721 than 706. The only answer that satisfies these criteria is C, 718.

The math way:

In this case we get to pick which data points we want to use. The closer the x values are to the target (16,000), the better our answer will be. So choose (x_a, y_a) to be (15,000, 721) and $(x_b, y_b$ to be (20,000, 706). When we plug in the values we know, the equation becomes:

$$y = 721 + \frac{(16{,}000 - 15{,}000)\ (706 - 721)}{(20{,}000 - 15{,}000)} = 721 + \frac{-1{,}000\ (15)}{5{,}000} = 721 - 3 = 718$$

We know you're thinking that you will never remember that formula, but it is really easier than it looks. The whole thing boils down to a simple ratio relationship:

If A is the distance between x_a and x_b, $(x_b - x_a)$,

B is the distance between y_a and y_b, $(y_b - y_a)$,

C is the distance between x_a and x, $(x - x_a)$, and

D is the distance between y_a and y, $(y - y_a)$,

Then the ratio of C to A has to be the same as the ratio of D to B. In other words: $C/A = D/B$ so $D = CB/A$, or

$y - y_a = (x - x_a)(y_b - y_a) / (x_b - x_a)$ $y = y_a + (x - x_a)(y_b - y_a) / (x_b - x_a)$

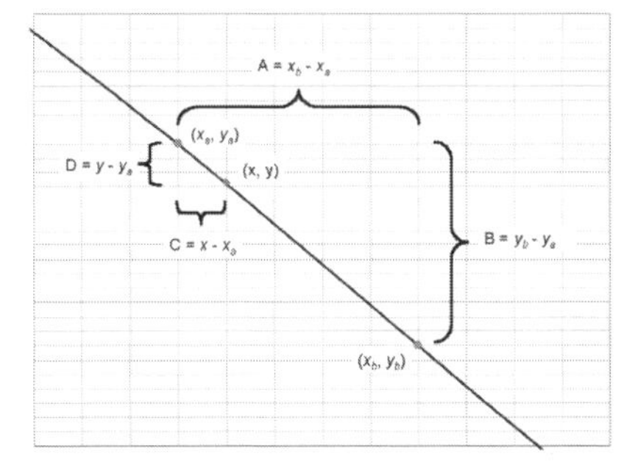

Did you notice that the speed of sound slowed down as your altitude increased? The speed of sound is a function of the density of the material it is going through. The less dense the material, the slower the speed of sound. Air is less dense at higher altitudes. That is why science types often get annoyed with space movies that show a space ship making a sound as it goes by. In space there is no air, so there is no sound. On the other hand, sound goes faster through water, which is denser than air, and even faster through wood or metal.

81. Make a Pitch

Here's a formula about sound and ultimately about music: $v = \lambda f$, where v is the speed of sound, λ (the Greek letter lambda) is the wavelength of the sound wave, and f is the frequency of the sound wave.

Jonathan plays middle C on the piano. He then plays the note C one octave up, which is higher in pitch (frequency) than middle C. Is the wavelength of the second note longer or shorter than middle C?

The answer is: Shorter.

First let's define what we're talking about:

- Sound will have a constant velocity through a material of constant density. The speed sound travels, is a function of the density of material it travels through, but not a function of the frequency or wavelength of the sounds.
- The wavelength (λ) is the distance between repeating units of a wave pattern.
- Frequency is the measurement of the number of times that a repeated event occurs per unit of time.

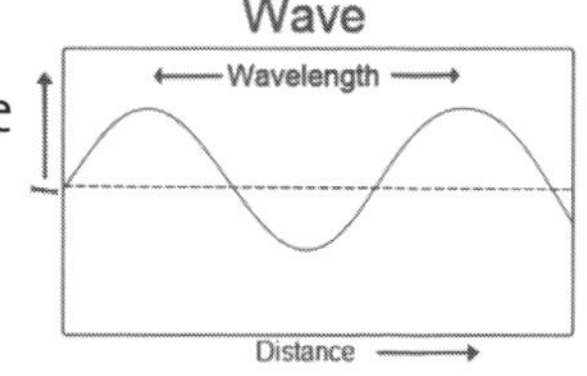

If the speed of sound (v) remains constant, when the frequency (f) of the sound goes up (providing a higher pitch), as it does in our case, then the wavelength must get smaller (shorter). In other words, there is an inverse relationship between f and λ—as one gets larger, the other must get smaller.

Waves of various frequencies; the waves on the bottom have higher frequencies than those at the top.

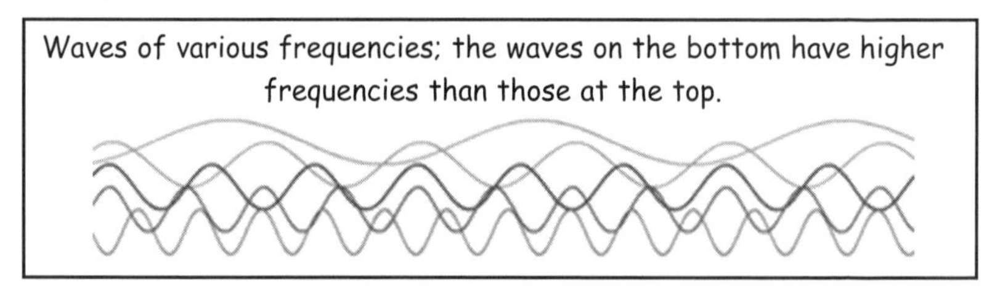

82. Tuning Up

Benjamin is tuning his piano. He measures the frequency of each note. He finds that the note A above middle C is tuned perfectly at 440 Hertz (Hz). He knows that in music, an octave is the interval between one musical note and another with half or double the frequency. In other words, the same note an octave higher would have double the frequency, and a note an octave lower would have half the frequency.

The A an octave above plays at a frequency of 900 Hz and the A an octave below plays at 200 HZ. In terms of percent error, which note is more in tune?

A. The A an octave below **C. They are both in tune**
B. The A an octave above **D. They are equally out of tune**

The answer is: B, the A an octave above

The formula to calculate percent error is $(V_{actual} - V_{expected}) \div V_{expected}$.

If the result is negative, it indicates that the actual value is lower than the expected value. In this question, we know that the A above middle C is in tune at 440 Hz; therefore, the A an octave above would be in tune at 880 Hz and the A an octave below would be in tune at 220 Hz.

The A an octave below measured at 200 Hz, so the percent error is:

$$\frac{(200-220)}{220} = \frac{-20}{220} = \frac{-1}{11} = 9\%$$

The A an octave above measured at 900 Hz, so the percent error is:

$$\frac{(900-880)}{880} = \frac{20}{880} = \frac{1}{44} = 2\%$$

83. Musical Mathematicians

Who on the following list of mathematicians (and who relied on math in their careers) also played a musical instrument?

A. Pythagoras **D. Augusta Ada Byron, Countess of Lovelace**
B. Albert Einstein **E. All of the above**
C. Enrico Fermi **F. None of the above**

NEED A CLUE? Whenever you think math, think music.

The answer is: E, all of the above

There is a long history of people of math and science who were also interested in and good at music. Here is a short list:

Pythagoras	Greek philosopher/Mathematician/Musician
Albert Einstein	Physicist/Violinist
Enrico Fermi	Physicist/Pianist
Richard Feynman	Physicist/Percussionist/Artist
Werner Von Braun	Rocket scientist/Piano and cello player
Edward Teller	Physicist/Pianist
Arthur Schawlow	Physicist/Clarinetist/Jazz fan
Albert Schweitzer	Humanitarian/Theologian/Missionary, medical doctor/World-class organist and Bach expert
Gerald Edelman	Nobel Laureate in Biology/Violinist
Augusta Ada Byron, Countess of Lovelace (daughter of the poet Lord Byron)	Mathematical visionary (credited with the invention of binary arithmetic)/Harpist

Many musicians have also had a keen interest in math and science. Here is another short list:

Peter I. Tchaikovsky	Composer/Mathematician
Alexander Borodin	Composer/Chemist
Fletcher Henderson	Jazz legend/Chemist
Charles Ives	Composer/Actuary
Victor Ewald	Composer/Engineer
Adolph Herseth	Legendary principal trumpet of Chicago Symphony Orchestra/Math degree
William Vacchiano	Principal trumpet of New York Philharmonic/NBC Orchestra/Studied accounting
Clifford Brown	Jazz trumpet legend/Majored in math/ Chess/expert
Ignance Jan Paderewski	Internationally acclaimed concert pianist/Ambassador from Poland to the United States, and President of the Polish parliament

84. Shapely Structures

Architects and engineers have used mathematical shapes to inspire their creations. Can you match the object with its inspiration?

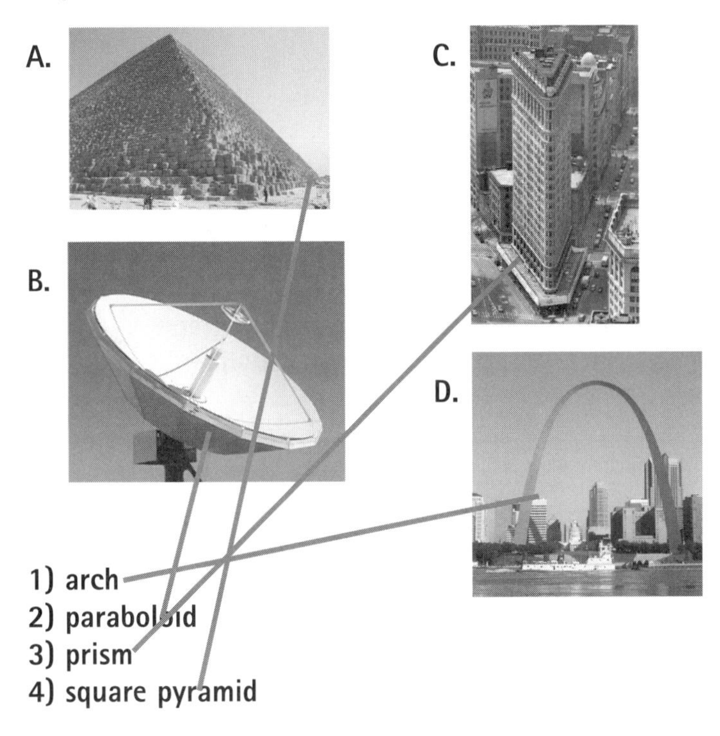

The answer is: A(4), B(2), C(3), D(1)

The Great Pyramid of Giza is the only one of the Seven Wonders of the Ancient World still standing at 4,500 years old. It is made up of over 2 million stone blocks each weighing 1.5 tons. Archeologists believe it took 100,000 people over 20 years to build. Its longevity can be attributed to its shape, which reinforces and stabilizes each side.

A satellite dish is in the shape of a paraboloid, or a parabola rotated about its central axis (a 3-D parabola). When signals hit the face of the dish, they are reflected and focused on the central antenna protruding from the middle. In a satellite dish, the paraboloid collects electromagnetic waves.

Buildings that fit onto a wedge-shaped plot of land take on the shape of a prism. A prism is a polyhedron that is made of two identical parallel polygons and connected by perpendicular, rectangular sides.

Arches have been used in buildings for thousands of years. Structurally, all the stones that make up an arch have to reinforce each other. That gives the arch significant strength.

85. The Big Chill

The equation to calculate wind chill (T_{wc}) is:

$$T_{wc} = 35.74 + 0.6215T_a - 35.75V^{0.16} + 0.4275T_aV^{0.16}$$

where T_{wc} and T_a (air temperature) are measured in °F, and velocity (or wind speed) in mph. Which line on the graph represents wind chill as a function of wind speed when air temperature is 20° F?

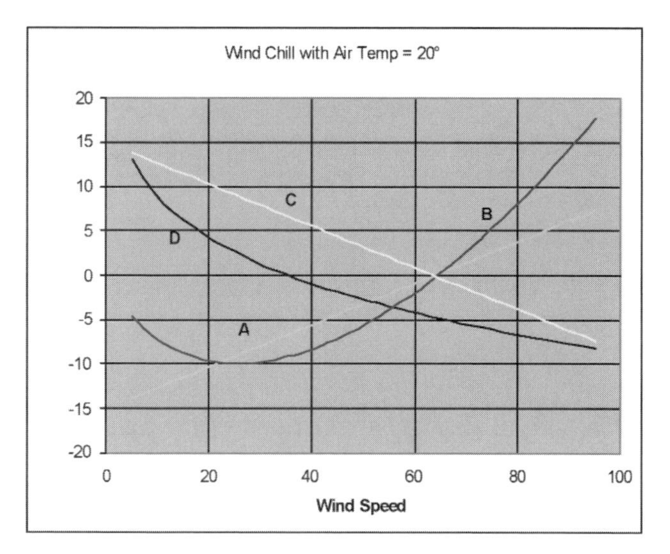

The answer is: D

Here's how to make the choice:

• Because there are terms in the formula that include V raised to a power, we know the two straight lines can't be correct. That leaves B & D.

- In the question, Ta is given as a constant: 20. So, the first two terms on the right hand side of the equation are also constant. In other words, they don't change as V changes and therefore will not help us figure out which curve is correct.
- Notice that V is raised to a power that is less than one (0.16 to be precise). When a function includes terms that are raised to a power greater than zero and less than one, that function will flatten out (become more horizontal) as the values entered into the function are raised. However, functions that include terms that are raised to powers greater than one will tend to become more vertical.
- In the graph, we can see that curve D is becoming more horizontal and B is becoming more vertical.
- Therefore, D must be the correct curve.

Hmm! Wind chill is a measure of how cold the air "feels" on exposed skin when both temperature and wind are taken into account. As the wind increases, heat leaves the body at a faster rate, driving down the body temperature. So the wind chill index shows the approximate temperature a human "feels."

Wind Chill	Cold Threat
41°F to 50°F	CHILLY. Generally unpleasant.
21°F to 40°F	COLD. Unpleasant.
1°F to 20°F	VERY COLD. Very unpleasant.
-19°F to 0°F	BITTER COLD. Frostbite possible. Exposed skin can freeze within 5 minutes.
-20°F to -69°F	EXTREMELY COLD. Frostbite likely. Exposed skin can freeze within 1 minute. Outdoor activity becomes dangerous.
-70°F and lower	FRIGIDLY COLD. Exposed skin can freeze in 30 seconds.

86. Watch for Falling Rocks

Two cavepeople, Ogg and Nahtogg, play a game in which they climb up on a cliff and drop rocks on the stuff that floats down the river. They know that, to hit a moving target, they have to drop the rock before the item is directly below them. They have been doing this so long that they have created a chart of how long it takes rocks to fall. When they climb up 100 feet, it takes 2.5 seconds for the rock to hit the object.
How long does it take for the rocks to hit the objects if they climb up 400 feet?

A. 3 seconds **C. 5 seconds**
B. 4 seconds **D. 6 seconds**

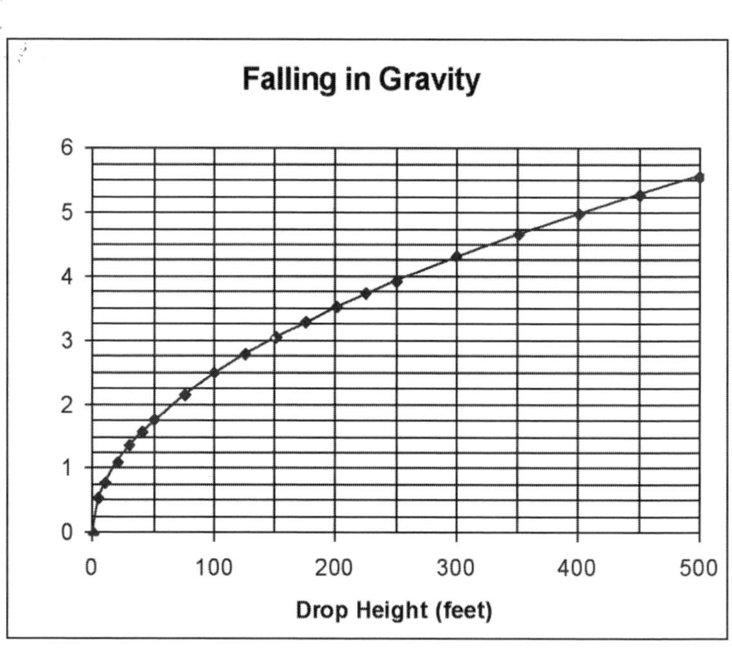

The answer is: C, 5 seconds

It is easy to find the solution if you happen to have this handy-dandy chart, but what if you forget it the one day you need to figure out how long it takes a penny to fall from the top of the Empire State Building? (Not that you would actually drop anything from there on purpose). To do this problem without a graph, you have to remember a formula. It's an easy one, and you may have noticed it in Question 52. One reason it is easy is because we stripped out the complicated stuff. It will give only an approximate answer, but that's okay for now.

The formula is, $t = \sqrt{h}/4$, where t is the falling time (in seconds) and h is the height (in feet) the object falls from.

Okay, how tall is the Empire State Building? Suppose you don't actually know. Suppose it is something like 100 stories, with each story about 10 feet high. So, h = 1,000, and the square root of 1,000 is... hmm, perhaps you don't know that either. But you do know that the square root of 900 is 30 and that 35 squared is 1225.

The square root of 1,000 is a lot closer to 30 than 35, so let's call it 31. Divide 31 by 4, and you get a smidge over 7.5. So it takes about 7.5 seconds for a penny to fall from the observation deck of the Empire State Building.

Author's Note: Perhaps you're insisting on the real answer, so you can tell how close to accurate your estimation is. We will spare you the real equation, which is a three-term quadratic, and just tell you the real numbers. The observation deck turns out to be 1,050 feet high (the official height of the building 1,454 feet, and the observation deck is on the 86th floor). It would actually take 8.08 seconds to fall that distance.

That is a little more than a 7% error. Typically for an estimate, within 10% is considered good, and within 5% is great. So we did well.

87. Shaking Things Up

Geologists use the Richter Magnitude Scale to compare the size and severity of earthquakes. The 1994 Northridge, California Earthquake was measured to be 6.5 on the Richter scale. The largest earthquake on record, the 1960 Great Chilean Earthquake, measured 9.5. About how much stronger was the Chilean earthquake?

A. 3 times stronger **C. 100 times stronger**
B. 10 times stronger **D. 1,000 times stronger**

The answer is: D, 1,000 times stronger. An earthquake that measures 9.5 is 1,000 times as powerful as a 6.5 earthquake.

The Richter Magnitude Scale measures how much the ground moves, and is based on a base 10 logarithmic scale. The values on the Richter scale are based on taking the logarithm of some value.

A logarithm is the mathematical operation that is the inverse (opposite) of exponentiation (raising a number, "b," to a power, "n," is written: b^n). The logarithm of a number, "x," in base "b" is the number n such that $x = b^n$. It is usually written as: $\log_b(x) = n$.

Using the Richter Magnitude Scale, a magnitude 4 quake is 10 times worse than a magnitude 3 quake, and a magnitude 5 quake is 10 times worse than a magnitude 4 quake, and so on.

88. Around the Sun

Which travels faster, the earth relative to the sun or the moon relative to the earth?

Hint: The earth is about 93 million miles from the sun, the moon is about 240,000 miles from the earth and pi is about 3.14.

The answer is: The earth relative to the sun

First, let's get some figures together. On average, the earth is 93 million miles from the sun and travels in an almost circular orbit. We will estimate the orbit to be circular with a radius of 9.3×10^7 miles (This number is written in scientific notation. Instead of writing 93,000,000, we recognize that $93{,}000{,}000 = 9.3 \times 10{,}000{,}000$ and 10,000,000 is the same as 10^7). Since we're estimating here, let make the radius 10^8. It's easier to work with.

It takes a year for the earth to travel around the sun. In that year, the earth travels $2\pi r$ miles (circumference of a circle). In our case that's $2\pi(10^8)$, which is about 6.2×10^8 miles. Finding the speed of the earth is easy; it's 6.2 x 108 miles per year. That's fine for now, but we'll have to convert it later.

Now, on to the moon:

The moon is about 240,000 miles from the earth and completes one orbit in about 27.3 days. The length of the orbit is $2\pi(2.4 \times 10^5)$ or approximately 1.5×10^6 miles. To find out how far the moon travels in one day, we can divide by 25 (If we were using a calculator we would use the real value of 27.3, but we're not so let's go with the easy calculation). Let's make it even a little easier by rewriting the distance as 150x104 ÷ 25 = $6\text{x}10^4$ miles per day.

Now we compare the moon's speed with the earth's speed: $6.2\text{x}10^8$ miles per year. We could divide $6.2\text{x}10^8$ by 365, but we don't have to. Because we are using scientific notation, we can see that the earth speed in miles per year is four orders of magnitude (10^4, or 10,000) times greater then the speed of the moon in miles per days. Ten-thousand divided by 365 is about 30. So, that means that the speed of the earth is close to 30 times the speed of the moon.

89. Seeing the Light

The primary colors for light are red, green and blue. The secondary colors (made by mixing two primary colors) are yellow, cyan and magenta. In light, to get yellow, you mix red and green. To get cyan, you mix blue and green. To get magenta, you mix red and blue.

Red, green and blue lights create the colors you see on a computer screen. The intensity of each color is rated from 0 to 255, where 0 is no light and 255 is full on. This is called the RGB scale, where R stands for red, G stands for green, and B stands for blue. In the RGB scale, the color white is R=255, G=255, B=255; black is R=0, G=0, B=0; red is R=255, G=0, B=0; yellow is R=255, G=255, B=0 and so on.

In HTML (the computer language used to create web pages), each color is identified in a special RGB format: #rrggbb. In this format, the first two digits after the # represent the intensity level for the red light, the next two digits represent the intensity level for the green light and the last two digits represent the intensity level for the blue light.

The intensity range is from 0 to 255, but the RGB format only leaves two digits for each color. How do we cram a three-digit number into two digits? We need to convert the decimal value for color intensity into base 16 (hexadecimal, or hex) (See question 97 for more on different number bases). In this number system, the "ones" place can hold the values 0 through 15 (base 10). The next place to the left is not the "tens place" as in base 10, but the sixteens place (because this is base 16—get it?) Now how do we put a 15 into the ones place? There are only 10 numbers developed for base 10 (0, 1, 2, 3, 4, 5, 6, 7, 8, 9). So, we improvise; we use letters. See the table below:

Base 10	0	1	2	3	4	5	6	7	8	9	10	11	12	13	14	15
Base 16	0	1	2	3	4	5	6	7	8	9	A	B	C	D	E	F

Match the RGB color code on the right with the most appropriate name on the left:

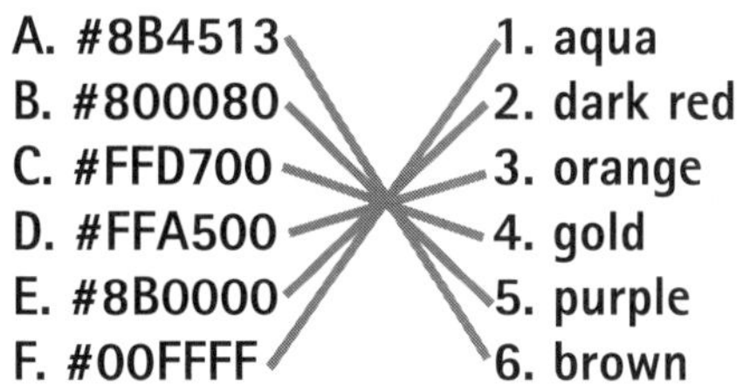

The answer is: A(6), B(5), C(4), D(3), E(2), F(1)

Let's go for the easy ones first:

- B has equal parts red and blue. That sounds a lot like purple (5).
- E has only red, but not at maximum intensity, so it must be dark red (2).
- F has no red, and the only color without any red would be aqua (1).
- That leaves A, C and D and the colors orange, gold and brown.
- Neither C nor D has any blue, only red and green. We know that yellow is made of red and green, with no blue. Therefore either C or D must be gold, which is like a dark yellow. But which one?
- The red values are the same, and the C has higher green intensity –so that should make it the gold (4).

• That leaves orange and brown. Brown has some cool color in it, so that means A must be brown (6).

• Therefore, D must be orange (3).

Here is a chart that breaks out the RGB scale into decimal values to make it easier to see:

RGB Code	Red	Green	Blue	Color
A. #8B4513	139	69	19	6. brown
B. #800080	128	0	128	5. purple
C. #FFD700	255	215	0	4. gold
D. #FFA500	255	165	0	3. orange
E. #8B0000	139	0	0	2. dark red
F. #00FFFF	0	255	255	1. aqua

Hmm! Most of us learn the color wheel very early in our education. We learn that the primary colors are red, yellow and blue. But the basis for that color wheel is mixing paints. If we mix colored lights, then the color wheel looks quite different.

Miscellaneous Answers

90. Cave Paper

Ogg the caveperson wants to decorate a cavern in the cave by putting up wallpaper. From floor to ceiling, the cavern is 8 feet tall.

Conveniently, the cavern is rectangular; except one wall is completely gone (it's the entrance.) The long walls are 15 feet, and the remaining short wall is 10 feet. The mud-colored wallpaper Ogg buys at Cave Depot is 3 feet wide, and each roll is 20 feet long. Assuming Ogg doesn't care if there are horizontal seams, how many rolls need to be purchased?

The answer is: 6

First, we need to figure out how much surface area needs to be covered:

- The sum of the lengths of the three walls to be covered is 15 feet + 15 feet + 10 feet = 40 feet.
- The height of the walls is 8 feet.

Therefore, the surface area is 40 feet x 8 feet = 320 square feet.

Next we figure out how much surface area each roll of wallpaper will cover:

Each roll is 3 feet wide and 20 feet long so it will cover 3 feet x 20 feet = 60 square feet.

Now we divide the surface area of the walls by the coverage area of the wallpaper and get 5.33. Therefore, Ogg needs to buy 6 rolls.

91. Cave Paper Continued

Interestingly enough, Nahtogg, the other caveperson, has a cavern the exact same size. Nahtogg also wants to wallpaper the cavern with the exact same kind of wallpaper as Ogg (actually, the choice of wallpaper is not surprising because it is the only kind Cave Depot carries).

The difference is that Nahtogg is very particular and does not want any horizontal seams in the middle of her walls. If a strip of wallpaper is not at least 8 feet long, she plans to throw it away. How many rolls of wallpaper does Nahtogg need to purchase?

The answer is: 7

Since we have to throw away lengths of wallpaper less than 8 feet long, if the length of a roll is evenly divisible by 8 then this question would have the same answer as the last one. However, 20 is not evenly divisible by 8 ($20 \div 8 = 2.5$). What we need to do now is to figure out the "effective" coverage of a roll of wallpaper, by adjusting the coverage values to reflect that we have to throw out part of the roll.

The effective roll length is $^4/_5 \times 20 = 16$ feet so the coverage becomes 16 feet x 3 feet = 48 square feet. Now we divide the surface area of the walls (320 square feet) by the coverage area of the wallpaper (48 square feet) and get 6.67. Therefore, Nahtogg needs to buy 7 rolls.

92. Pet Pen

Mal builds a rectangular pen to hold his pet snails. Then Mal decides to make one side of the pen longer by $^1/_3$. By what percentage should Mal reduce the other dimension to keep the area of the pen the same?

The answer is: 25%.

Here's how to figure it out:

When you increase one dimension by $^1/_3$, the percentage change is +33.3%.

To calculate the new length you use the formula L(1+c) where L is original length and c is the percent change expressed as a decimal number.

To convert 33.3% into a decimal number, divide by 100. So, 33.3% becomes 0.333.

Therefore, the equation becomes L(1+0.333) or 1.333L.

We know that the original area A = LW, where L = length & W = width.

Now the new length is 1.333L so we know that A = LW = 1.333L(W(1+c)), c is the change in the width.

We can cancel out the LW from both sides and get 1 = 1.333(1+c). We divide by 1.333 and get .75 = 1+c, so c = -.25

So, why is it that when you increase one dimension by $^1/_3$, you decrease the other dimension by only _ to keep the area the same? The answer is clear if we use fractions instead of decimals. Let's look at it this way: $LW = (1+{}^1/_3)L \times (1-{}^1/_4)W = {}^4/_3\, L \times {}^3/_4 W = {}^4/_3\, ({}^3/_4)LW = LW$.

93. Weather or Not

Your mom tells you to pack for a surprise adventure. The one hint she gives you is to pack the type of clothes suitable for a place where the daytime temperature will be about 30°C. What should you pack for your afternoon adventure?

☞ **A. Tank tops and light pants or shorts**
B. Flannel shirts and jeans
C. Wool sweaters, corduroy pants and a warm jacket

The answer is: A, tank tops and light pants or shorts (30°C = 86°F).

There are several different ways to indicate temperature. In the United States, the most common way is on the Fahrenheit scale (written as °F). On this scale water freezes at 32°F, water boils at 212°F and average normal body temperature is 98.6°F.

Most of the rest of the world, however, uses the Celsius, or Centigrade, scale (written as °C). In this system, water freezes at 0°C, water boils at 100°C and average normal body temperature is 37°C.

Here is the equation to convert from a temperature on the Celsius scale (C) to a temperature on the Fahrenheit scale (F):

$F = {}^{9}/_{5} \times C + 32$

To convert from 30°C to °F, the equation is:

$F = ({}^{9}/_{5})\ 30 + 32 = 54 + 32 = 86°F.$

A more user-friendly way to write the equation is:

$F = 2(C - .1C) + 32.$

SHORTCUT: About now you're thinking that the conversion is hard to remember. Good news! There is an easier equation used to estimate the conversion from Celsius to Fahrenheit. It is: 2C + 30. So you can estimate that 30°C would be near 90°F, definitely not wool sweater weather! The estimate works best between 0°C and 30°C, which is the range in which most of us live. But use the real conversion equation for science experiments.

94. Temperature Crossover

The boiling point of water is 100°C or 212°F. The freezing point of water is 0°C or 32°F. Is there a temperature value that is the same on both the Celsius and Fahrenheit scales?

The answer is: Yes, -40

We can figure this out two ways, the first by using algebra and the second by plotting. To use algebra, we must first recall the conversion to Fahrenheit: $F = {}^{9}/_{5} \times C + 32$

Since we are looking for the value of C that equals the value of F we can just assign C = F in the equation, which means we can substitute C for F. The equation becomes $F = {}^{9}/_{5}F + 32$.

That simplifies to $(1 - {}^{9}/_{5})F = 32$ or $F = 32 \div -({}^{4}/_{5})$, so F = -40.

The graphical solution requires us to plot two equations on the same axes; namely, $F = {}^{9}/_{5} \times C + 32$ and $C = (F-32) \times {}^{5}/_{9}$.

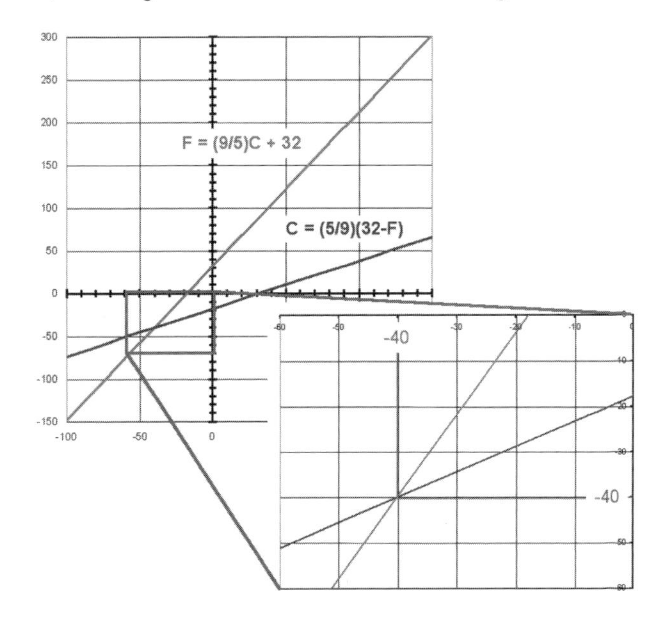

The second equation is the conversion from Celsius to Fahrenheit and comes from using algebra as follows.

$F = {}^{9}/_{5} \times C + 32 \quad F-32 = {}^{9}/_{5}C \quad C = ({}^{5}/_{9})(F-32)$

When we plot both equations, we can see that they intersect at –40.

Hmm! The Celsius temperature scale has numbers that seem to make sense and are easy to remember (0 for freezing and 100 for boiling). The Fahrenheit scale uses less obvious values (32 for freezing and 212 for boiling). Why? One of the most common theories is that Gabriel Fahrenheit attempted to calculate body temperature at 100 and the freezing point of a water/salt solution (which freezes at a lower temperature than pure water) to be zero. Then he played around so that there would be 64 even increments between body temperature and pure water's freezing point. Anders Celsius made his scale 18 years later, in 1742, and used more straightforward values.

95. Flip a Coin

When your friend is bored, he has a habit of flipping a coin into the air, catching it and calling out whether it landed on heads or tails. Today, he is bored. You have heard him call out "Heads, tails, tails, heads, heads, heads." He then says to you, "I just flipped three heads in a row. What is the chance that my next flip will be heads?" Is it...

A. 25% **C. 75%**

☞ **B. 50%** **D. 100%**

The answer is: B, 50%

Coins do not have memory. The probability of flipping a coin heads-side up (or tails-side up for that matter) never changes, regardless of the number of previous flips. There is always a 50-50 chance of the coin landing on heads.

On the other hand, suppose you have a bag filled with 100 marbles where 99 are black and 1 is white. The likelihood of drawing a white marble would change with every draw, assuming that any marble drawn is not put back in the bag.

96. Betting on the Square

Barnabas is taking a timed math test, without a calculator. He comes to the last problem: 36^2. Barnabas is very slow doing multiplication with more than one digit, and he has less than one minute left. Do you think he will be able to solve the last problem in the time he has left?

The answer is: Yes.

Test Taking Skill! Barnabas didn't sweat it because he knew a trick, and now you'll know it, too! Let's go through it graphically first. The graphical representation of 2^2 is a square with two units per side.

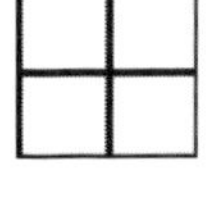

You can count the number of small squares and see that 2x2 = 4.

Doing the same thing for 3^2, you get a 3 by 3 square.

You can count the squares to find that $3^2 =$ 3x3 = 9.

If we place the 2x2 square over the 3x3 square so that the lower left-hand corners coincide, you get:

From this picture you can see that there are two small squares to the right of the 2x2 square and 3 on the top row, so $2^2 + 2 + 3 = 3^2$.

The general formula is:

The square of any integer M is: $M^2 = (M-1)^2+(M-1)+M$.

For example $3^2 = (3-1)^2 + (3-1) + 3 = 2^2 + 2 + 3 = 9$.

Let's try this out on something a little harder like 36^2 - Holy Toledo! – That's a tough one. I don't know what 35^2 is off the top of my head. The good news is that we have a trick for that too.

SHORTCUT: There is a shortcut to find the square of any number that ends in a 5, it works like this: The last two numbers in the solution will always be 25, so you can write them down first. To calculate the remaining part of the number we look at the number created when we discard the final 5 (in the one's place), we'll call it N. (You can calculate it by taking the original number, subtracting 5 and dividing by 10.

For example, 35 becomes $(35 - 5)\div10 = 3)$. In this case N = 3. (If we started with 205 then N would equal 20.) Now we take N and multiply it by N+1 and then by 100. In this case $100 \times N \times (N+1) = 100 \times 3 \times 4 = 1200$.

This product is added to the initial 25 (1200+25 =1225). If the number to be squared is 205 then the equation is $20 \times 21 \times 100 + 25 = 42{,}000 + 25 = 42{,}025$.

So, back to 36^2. Based on the equation above, $36^2 = 35^2 + 35 + 36 = 1225 + 71 = 1296$.

97. Covering All the Bases

Match these multiplication problems with the base number system they were calculated in:

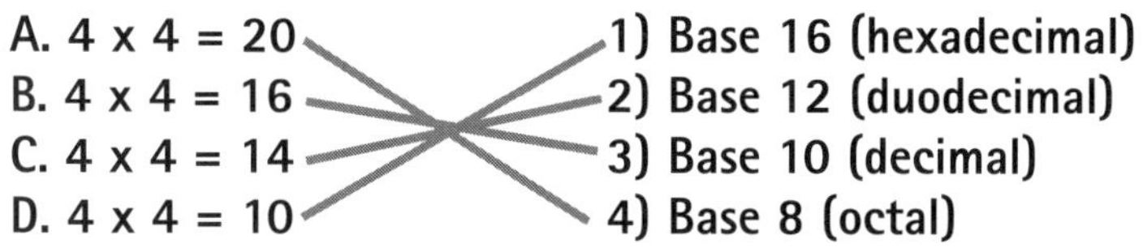

Answer: A (4), B (3), C (2), D (1)

Working in different number bases can be useful. So a basic understanding of how it's done is worth the risk of occasional confusion.

These days, the most common number system is base 10, which is the one you ordinarily use for your number needs.

Base 2, also called binary, is for computers and has only two digits, zero & one.

Base 16 (typically referred to as hex, or hexadecimal) is probably the next most common base system, also for computers. (See question 89.) In the past, computers also used base 8. However, it is seen less often these days.

In base 10 (the base you know and love), 4 x 4 = 16. (For clarity, write 16 in base 10 as 16_{10}.). Therefore we know that B matches with 3. Our job is to convert 16_{10} into the other three bases and see how the numbers look.

So here's a review of number systems:

Start with base 10. We know that the first place (the right most before the decimal point) is called the ones place and can hold any number from 0 to 9.

The next place to the left is the tens place, and its value is 10 times the number contained there.

Then there's the hundreds place, the thousands place, etc. We can make the names more general by recognizing that $10^0 = 1$, $10^1 = 10$, $10^2 = 100$, etc. Do you see the pattern?

It turns out this pattern holds for all bases. For example, the places in base 8 are $8^0 = 1$, $8^1 = 8$, $8^2 = 64$, $8^3 = 512$. Also for base 8 we only use the digits 0-7.

Now we need to convert 16_{10} into base 8:

First, divide 16 by 8 to get 2. This means that there are two eights in 16. We can write the number as 20_8 (that's 2 eights, zero ones), so that means that A matches with 4. Next, we do the same thing for base 12. We divide 16 by 12 and get 1 with a remainder of 4. That means that we have one twelve and four ones or 14_{12}, so C matches 2. That leaves D to match 1, but to satisfy our mathematical curiosity; we divide 16 by 16 and get 1 so the result is 10_{16}.

98. Exceptional Student Combinations

Every day in math class, the teacher picks the Exceptional Student of the Day and puts the name in a bowl. Each Friday the teacher picks 2 names out of the bowl for a prize. If your name is on both tickets, you get a homework pass that gives you the privilege of not doing one homework assignment. At the end of the first week, there are 5 names in the bowl and 2 of them are yours. What are the chances of you getting the homework pass?

The answer is: 10%

The probability of pulling your name on the first draw is 2 out of 5, or $^2/_5$, or 40%.

On the second draw, the chance of pulling your name is 1 out of 4 (four, because a name was already taken out and not returned), or $^1/_4$, or 25%.

The probability of both names being yours is the probability of the first name being yours multiplied by the probability of the second name being yours: .40 x .25 = .10, or 10%.

Here's another way to solve this:

In this question there are five possible choices for the first draw and four for the second, etc., so we start with 5!, which represents all the possible choices (see question 48). However, in this case we only care about two draws, not the five that 5! represents. Out of five draws, we take two, and that leaves three, so we need to divide 5! by 3! ($\frac{5!}{3!}$). That means that there are 20 different possible ways the names can be drawn ($\frac{120}{6} = 20$).

This is called the permutation of 5 things, taken 2 at a time. Sometimes you see it written as 5^P2.

The general equation of n^Pm is $\frac{n!}{(n-m)!}$, Where n is the number of elements available for selection and m is the number of elements to be selected (m must be less than or equal to n). The symbol ^{P} denotes the operator for permutation. So 5^P2 is interpreted as "How many different ways can someone order two items selected from a set of five items when the order of things matter."

Whoops! This is not the answer we are looking for! A permutation is an "ordered list." That means that what order the tickets are drawn in makes a difference. In this case we don't care about the order the names are drawn. That means that there are fewer combinations. A mathematical combination is an unordered list.

To turn the permutation n^Pm into a combination n^Cm, divide n^Pm by m!. The equation is $n^Cm = \frac{n!}{m!(n-m)!}$, where n is the number of elements available for selection and m is the number of elements to be selected (m must be less than or equal to n). The symbol C denotes the operator for combination. So 5^C2 is interpreted as "How many different ways can someone order two items selected from a set of five items when the order of things does not matter." Or, in our case, we get $\frac{5!}{2!\,(3!)} = \frac{120}{12} = 10$ possible combinations. Of the 10 combinations, only one is your name both times. So your chance of winning is one-tenth, 10%, or 1 out of 10.

99. Too Much Tunafish

Baozhai has a new digital music player, called a pPod. He puts 100 of his favorite songs on it. Baozhai chooses the function so that his pPod will play the songs in random order. Baozhai is concerned when out of the first 10 random songs, the song "Tunafish" is played three times. What should Baozhai do?

A. Put in a new battery

B. Add more songs

C. Return to the store for a replacement

☞ **D. Nothing—it is working fine.**

The answer is: D, nothing—it is working fine

The pPod plays the songs randomly, which means each time it electronically decides which song to play, it uses an algorithm to pick the new song. The algorithm does not keep track of history. It simply picks a new song to play. In this case there are 100 songs, so the machine assigns each song a number between 1 and 100. Then it picks one of the numbers randomly, without regard to what it has played previously.

100. Electoral College

The Electoral College is charged with electing the President and Vice President of the United States. Each of the 50 states is allocated electoral votes equal to the number of representatives in Congress (number in the House + the number in the Senate). The District of Columbia also has 3 electoral votes. There are 435 Representatives + 100 Senators + 3 DC votes = 538 total electoral votes.

As a rule of thumb, the electors from each state all vote for the Presidential candidate who had the most votes in their state. Whichever candidate has at least 270 electoral votes is elected president. This chart shows the number of electoral votes per state:

What is the fewest number of states required to reach 270 electoral votes?

A. 6 C. 16

☞ B. 11 D. 26

State	Electoral Votes	State	Electoral Votes	State	Electoral Votes
Alabama	9	Kentucky	8	North Dakota	3
Alaska	3	Louisiana	9	Ohio	20
Arizona	10	Maine	4	Oklahoma	7
Arkansas	6	Maryland	10	Oregon	7
California	55	Massachusetts	12	Pennsylvania	21
Colorado	9	Michigan	17	Rhode Island	4
Connecticut	7	Minnesota	10	South Carolina	8
D.C.	3	Mississippi	6	South Dakota	3
Delaware	3	Missouri	11	Tennessee	11
Florida	27	Montana	3	Texas	34
Georgia	15	Nebraska	5	Utah	5
Hawaii	4	Nevada	5	Vermont	3
Idaho	4	New Hampshire	4	Virginia	13
Illinois	21	New Jersey	15	Washington	11
Indiana	11	New Mexico	5	West Virginia	5
Iowa	7	New York	31	Wisconsin	10
Kansas	6	North Carolina	15	Wyoming	3

The answer is: B, 11

That's 11 states like this:

State	Electoral Votes
California	55
Florida	27
Georgia	15
Illinois	21
Michigan	17
New Jersey	15
New York	31
North Carolina	15
Ohio	20
Pennsylvania	21
Texas	34
Total	271

Hmm! In theory, a candidate could win each of these states by a single vote, have no votes in any of the other 39 states or Washington, DC, and still be elected President of the United States.

101. Census Consensus

As of the last census, the town of Gooberville has 855 people, 367 households and 230 families residing in the town. The population density was 842.2/mi^2 (323.6/km^2). There were 411 housing units at an average density of 404.8/mi^2 (155.6/km^2). There were 678 dogs, 300 cats and 104 birds owned as pets. Based on this information, which one of these statements is true?

☞ **A. Gooberville is larger than one square mile**

B. Every household in Gooberville owns at least one dog

C. There are no people that live alone in Gooberville

D. Every family owns at least one cat

The Answer is: A, Gooberville is larger than one square mile

Population density is a measure of population per unit area. In Gooberville, we know there were 855 people living in town. However, the population density was 842.2 people per square mile. Remember population density is an average and gives no real indication of where, specifically, anyone lives within the area.

If Gooberville took up an area of exactly 1 mi^2 and 855 people lived there, the population density would be 855/mi^2. Because the population density is less than the population, we can conclude that Gooberville must be larger than one square mile.

The statistics give only the number of dogs and cats, and no indication of who owns them. While statements B and D might be true, we can't know it for sure based on the information given.

The information also states that there are 367 households and 230 families. Assume that a family is two or more people who live together and are related in some way. The fact that there are 137 more households than families indicates that those 137 households are composed of only one person or groups of people who are not related. In either case, we cannot know for sure that no one lives alone.

Bonus Answers

1. Monthly Lunch

A group of 7 friends go out to lunch every month. All the friends pay for their own meals, unless it is someone's birthday that month. The birthday boy or girl does not pay to eat because the rest of the group pays for his or her meal. Their favorite restaurant has a large selection of lunch specials that all cost the same. With tax and tip, each person pays exactly $12.00.

It was noticed that certain months don't have any birthdays, some only have one birthday, and some have two or more birthdays.

One friend also noted that the people who don't share their birthday month pay more money in the course of a year than those who do share their birthday month. What formula should be used to be sure that, over the course of a year, each person pays the same amount?

The answer is: $m(1+\frac{b}{f})$ for those not celebrating birthdays, and $m(\frac{b-1}{f})$ for those celebrating birthdays.

The problem with the original way the lunches were paid is that for months where there was more than one birthday, the birthday people didn't pay anything, when rightly they should have paid a portion of the other birthday person's lunch. Over the course of the year, everybody should pay for 11 of their own meals—plus 1/6 of each of 6 other people's meals—for a total of 12 meals.

During a month when it is not your birthday, you must pay for your own meal (to make the formula general, let's call the price of the meal m) plus $\frac{b}{6}$ of a meal, where b is the number of birthdays that month. The formula is therefore, $m(1+\frac{b}{6})$.

During a month when it is your birthday, the formula is the same—except you don't pay for your own lunch. The formula is: $m(\frac{b-1}{6})$. You need to subtract 1 from b so that you don't pay for 1/6 of one of the birthday lunches (your own). We can make the formula even more general by replacing the 6 with the variable f, which represents the total number of friends in the group. The formulas become:

- $m(1+\frac{b}{f})$ for those not celebrating birthdays, and
- $m(\frac{b-1}{f})$ for those celebrating birthdays.

2. Freedom the Frog

Freedom the frog has a peculiar habit. When he jumps, he can leap halfway across the room. But when he makes his next leap, he leaps only half the remaining distance, and with the next leap, again, jumps only half the remaining distance. Given enough time, will Freedom ever make it out of the room?

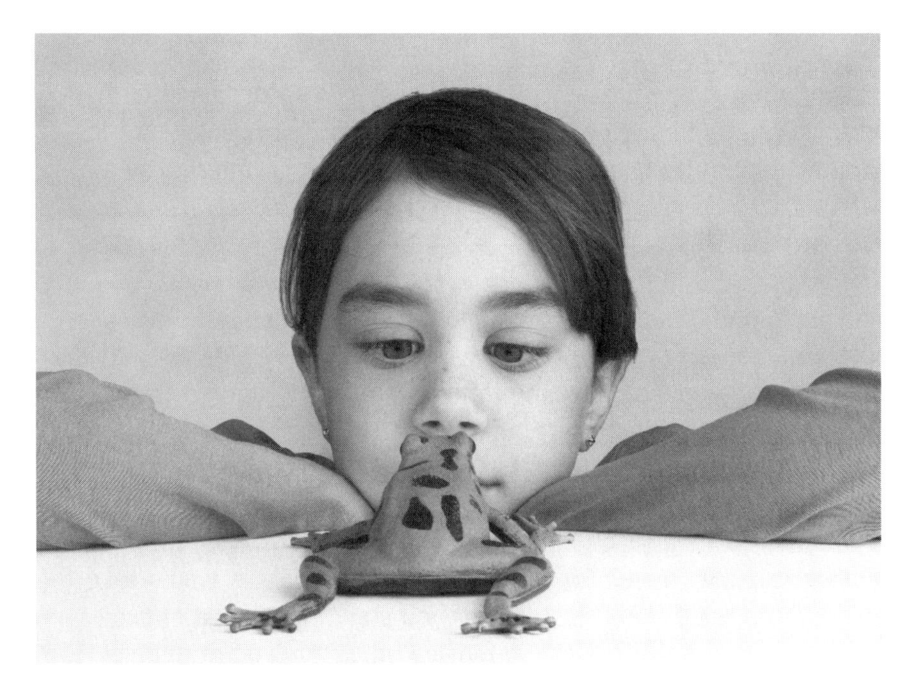

The answer is: Yes, given enough time.

Let's assume the room is only one meter wide. Then the first jump covers $^1/_2$ meter, the second jump covers $^1/_4$ meter, the third jump $^1/_8$ meter, and so on.

Here's the formula:

$$S = \frac{1}{2} + \frac{1}{4} + \frac{1}{8} + \frac{1}{16} + \frac{1}{32} + \ldots$$

Notice that every term is the preceding term multiplied by _ . This is called a "geometric series," and as long as the ratio between terms is greater than -1 and less than 1, you can calculate the sum.

So multiply both sides of the equation by the ratio 1/2, and you get:

$$\frac{1}{2}S = \frac{1}{4} + \frac{1}{8} + \frac{1}{16} + \frac{1}{32} + \frac{1}{64} + \ldots$$

If we line up the two equations and move the terms of the second equation one place to the right, we get this curious set of equations:

$$S = \frac{1}{2} + \frac{1}{4} + \frac{1}{8} + \frac{1}{16} + \frac{1}{32} + \ldots$$

$$\frac{1}{2}S = \quad\quad \frac{1}{4} + \frac{1}{8} + \frac{1}{16} + \frac{1}{32} + \frac{1}{64} + \ldots$$

Each term in the second equation lines up with the same term in the first equation (when both go out to infinity). If we subtract the second equation from the first, almost all the terms cancel, leaving: $S-1/2\ S=1/2,\ S=1$

That means: $1 = \frac{1}{2} + \frac{1}{4} + \frac{1}{8} + \frac{1}{16} + \frac{1}{32} + \ldots$

and Freedom makes it one meter, and out of the room, after an infinite number of jumps

How can a frog make an infinite number of jumps without taking an infinite amount of time? Since the jumps get smaller and smaller, the time it takes to make the jumps should also get smaller and smaller. So, if the first jump takes $^1/_2$ second the next would take $^1/_4$ second, then $^1/_8$ second and so on. So we can solve for the time the same way we solved for the distance. In this case it would take 1 second to go the 1 meter distance. If you stand at the end of the room with the stopwatch and you yelled go, at the end of one second, Freedom would be at your feet – an infinite number of jumps in a finite amount of time. Zeno of Elea was the first person to discuss the nature of this paradox.

3. Counting in Binary

Ogg the caveperson is in charge of keeping track of the tribe's collection of rocks. This is an important responsibility, so Ogg is working on a way to keep a running count of the rocks. The problem is that writing has not yet been invented, so the only way Ogg has to keep a record is by counting on his fingers. If the tribe starts out with 837 rocks, what is the fewest number of hands Ogg needs to start tracking the 837 rocks?

The answer is: 2

Everyone knows that there are five fingers on each hand so you divide 837 by 5 and get 167.4, which is rounded up to 168 hands. How can we claim that the minimum number of hands is two? The answer is one word: binary.

Counting in binary (or base two) is a good skill to master. Representing a number in binary requires only two numerals (0 and 1). Therefore, we can let each finger represent one digit of a binary number. A raised finger represents a one (1), and a lowered finger represents a zero (0). In this way, it is possible to count on your fingers up to 1,023 ($2^9 + 2^8 + 2^7 + 2^6 + 2^5 + 2^4 + 2^3 + 2^2 + 2^1 + 2^0$).

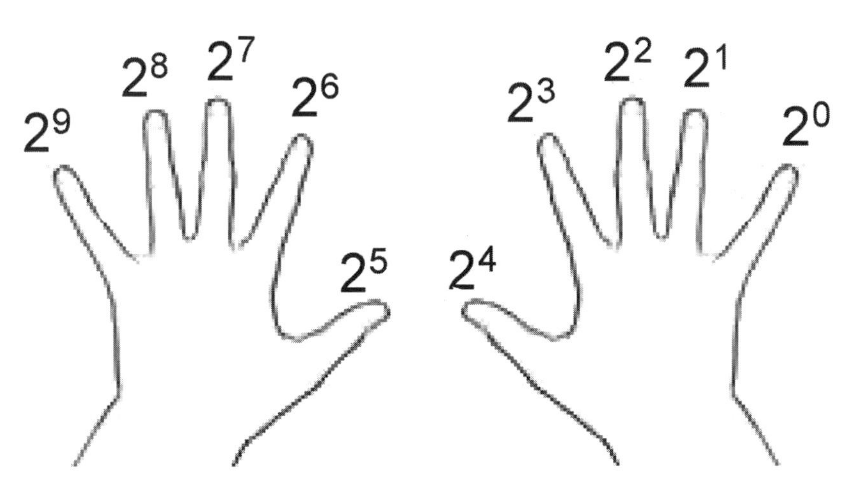

4. Road Trip

Ella and her family are going on a car trip. They plan to visit the towns neighboring Gooberville, her home town. Using the map and mileage chart, plan a route that starts and ends in Gooberville, requires the least amount of driving, and will take Ella and her family to each of the other towns only once.

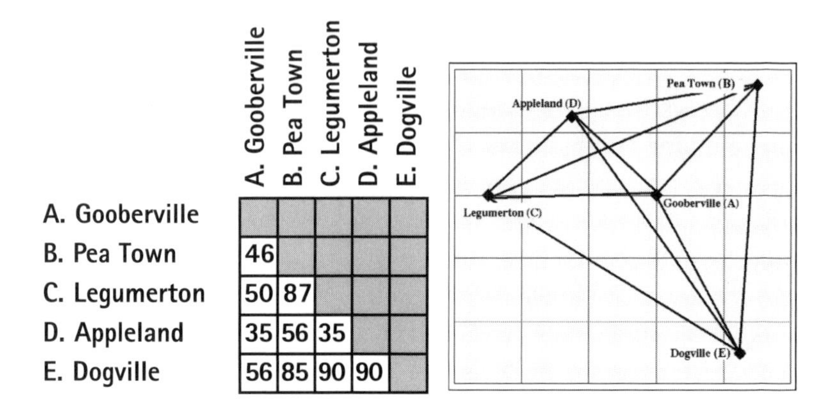

	A. Gooberville	B. Pea Town	C. Legumerton	D. Appleland	E. Dogville
A. Gooberville					
B. Pea Town	46				
C. Legumerton	50	87			
D. Appleland	35	56	35		
E. Dogville	56	85	90	90	

The answer is: A,E,B,D,C,A (and A,C,D,B,E,A gives the identical answer)

Without a map, this would be very difficult.

With the aid of the map (low on details as it is) and the mileage chart, we can make the following observations.

- Dogville is 90 miles from both Legumerton and Appleland.
- Legumerton and Appleton are relatively close to each other.

We can infer from the fact that Gooberville (A), our starting point, is closer to Appleland (D) and Dogville (E) than these two places are to each other. They are on opposite sides of Gooberville (A). We can confirm that by looking at the map.

This tells us that starting towards Dogville (E), Appleland (D) or Legumerton (C) will likely give us good results. The key to deciding which city to drive to first lies in noticing that the longest routes are BC, BE, CE & DE. The more of these routes you avoid, the shorter the overall path.

The easiest one to avoid is BC (87 miles). If you drive CD to DB (or vice versa), you will see three cities and drive 91 miles, as opposed to driving 87 miles and only seeing two cities. If you choose the CDB path, you can limit your trips by driving from A to E (at the start of your trip) or E to A (at the end of the trip).

The rest is crunching the numbers.

5. Funny Bunnies

Leo read an ad in Cabin Foci Weekly about rabbits. The ad said that if you buy one pair of newborn rabbits, then
1) They become fertile in two months.
2) Once they are fertile, every month they will become parents of a new pair.

Before you know it, Leo is the proud owner of a pair of newborn rabbits. Here's how time progresses:

- At the beginning of the 1st month, he has one pair.
- At the beginning of the 2nd month, he still has one pair.
- At the beginning of the 3rd month, just as the ad said, there are now two pairs of rabbits.
- 4th month, the first pair gives birth to another pair making three pairs.
- At the beginning of the 5th month, Leo counts 5 pairs of rabbits, and realizes the set born in the 3rd month must have given birth as well.

Leo makes a chart to figure out how many pairs of rabbits he will have at the end of the year:

Beginning of Month Number	Number of Pairs
1	1
2	1
3	2
4	3
5	5
6	
7	
8	
9	
10	
11	
12	

How many pairs will there be at the end of the year?

The answer is: 144.

Look back at the chart in month 4. There are 3 pairs. One pair was new that month, while the other 2 pairs are at least 2 months old. Since they were born in month 3, they are old enough to produce another pair each.

The number of pairs in month 5 will equal the number of pairs from month 4 plus the new pairs from the rabbit born in month 3, or 3 + 2 = 5. The pattern is then:

1, 1, 2, 3, 5, 8, 13, 21, 34, 55, 89, 144, 233, 377, 610, ...

With all these pairs, I think Leo's going to end up with a full house!

The first Western mathematician to discuss this series was Leonardo of Pisa, also known as Fibonacci, and the series is called the Fibonacci series.

Amazingly enough, Fibonacci series appear frequently in nature. The number of petals on a flower tends to be a Fibonacci number:

- 3 petals: trillium, lily, iris
- 5 petals: buttercup, wild rose, larkspur, columbine (aquilegia)
- 8 petals: delphiniums
- 13 petals: black-eyed Susan, corn marigold, cineraria
- 21 petals: aster, Shasta daisy, chicory
- 34 petals: field daisies
- 55, 89 petals: michaelmas daisies, the asteraceae family

Fibonacci numbers also appear in the arrangement of leaves on a stem, the number of spirals on a pinecone or sunflower, and the bumps on a pineapple.

"Yes, we have *Chicken Soup for the Math Teacher's Soul.* The price is $\$475 \div 23 \text{ x } .018^2 - Y^3 + 4X \div \$73.99999 + 2$."

Science, Naturally! wishes to thank our wonderful editorial staff whose enthusiasm, eagle eyes and critical reading helped shape this into the fun and wonderful book that it is!

Jennifer Zoon, Kensington, MD
Danielle Donaldson, Norco, CA
Nora Goldman, Philadelphia, PA
Andrea W. Bailey, Washington, DC
Kristin Francoz, New York, NY
Casey Heilig, Washington, DC
Stine Bauer Dahlberg, Washington, DC
Molly Katharine Nelson, Washington, DC
Elaine Nicole Simeon, San Francisco, CA
Morgan Haronian, Westerly, RI

Photo and Illustration Credits

Cover, Book Design, Charts, Tables and Section Illustrations by Andrew Barthelmes, Peekskill, NY

Cover images provided from:

H. Michael Mogil, Naples, FL
Carl Mehler, Pasadena, CA
Kenneth G. Libbrecht, Washington, DC
Stephen Strathdee, istockphoto.com
Debi Bishop, istockphoto.com
Dainis Derics, istockphoto.com
Geoff Kuchera, istockphoto.com

Page 14 Cartoon by Sydney Harris, reprinted with permission
Page 66 Cartoon by Randy Glasbergen, reprinted with permission
Page 68 Graphic by Will Layman, reprinted with permission
Page 74 Photo by Gordon Swanson; dreamstime.com
Page 79 Photo by Undisclosed; istockphoto.com
Page 81 Graphic by Mark Zev, Chatsworth, CA
Page 86 Photo by Jonathon Ross; dreamstime.com
Page 90 Photo by Dawn Hudson; dreamstime.com
Page 92 Photo by Monkey Business Images; dreamstime.com
Page 94 Photo by Undisclosed; dreamstime.com
Page 99 Photo by Peter Jobst; dreamstime.com
Page 101 Photo by Paval Jedlicka; dreamstime.com
Page 102 Photo by Undisclosed; dreamstime.com
Page 105 Photo by Kathleen Barthelmes, Peekskill, NY
Page 107 Photo by Undisclosed; dreamstime.com
Page 110 Photo by Rodney Hobart; dreamstime.com
Page 113 Photo by Amy Myers; dreamstime.com
Page 114 Photo by Undisclosed; dreamstime.com
Page 115 Photo by Kathy Winn; dreamstime.com
Page 116 Photo by Undisclosed; dreamstime.com
Page 118 Photo by Galina Barskaya; dreamstime.com
Page 119 Photo by Hasbro, Inc., reprinted with permission
Page 122 Photo by Chris Brignell, dreamstime.com
Page 126 Photo by Undisclosed; dreamstime.com
Page 127 Photo by John Anderson; dreamstime.com
Page 128 Photo by Olga Bogatyrenko; dreamstime.com
Page 132 Photo by Undisclosed; dreamstime.com
Page 134 Photo by Dmitry Kutlayev; dreamstime.com
Page 137 Photo by Undisclosed; dreamstime.com
Page 146 Photo by Torch Desings; dreamstime.com
Page 157 Photo by Matthew Apps; dreamstime.com
Page 158 Photo by Hepatus Photo; istockphoto.com
Page 159 Photo by Undisclosed; istockphoto.com
Page 164 Photo by Christos Georghio; dreamstime.com
Page 165 Photo by Ziva Kirn; istockphoto.com
Page 167 Photo by undisclosed; dreamstime.com
Page 169 Photo by Suspended Image; istockphoto.com
Page 172 Photo by Monkey Business Images; istockphoto.com
Page 179 Photo by Undisclosed; dreamstime.com
Page 181 Photo by Cory Thoman, dreamstime.com
Page 185 Cartoon by Randy Glasbergen, reprinted with permission

Math Resources

Organizations

American Mathematical Society (www.ams.org)
AMS aims to promote mathematical research, strengthen education and foster awareness and appreciation of mathematics.
(800) 321-4AMS
ams@ams.org

American Statistical Association (www.amstat.org)
ASA was founded in 1839 to foster excellence in the use and application of statistics.
(888) 231-3473
asainfo@amstat.org

Association of Mathematics Teacher Educators (www.amte.net)
AMTE's mission is to promote the improvement of education, in higher education.
(619) 594-3971
nbezuk@mail.sdsu.edu

Association for Women in Mathematics (www.awm-math.org)
AWM is dedicated to encouraging women and girls in the mathematical sciences.
(703) 934-0163
awm@awm-math.org

Australian Mathematical Society (www.austms.org.au)
AMS provides information about mathematics in Australia including publications, events and careers.
+(61) 2-6125-8922
office@austms.org.au

Bernoulli Society for Math Statistics and Probability
(htt//isi.cbs.nl/BS/bshome.htm)
The Society was founded in 1975 to promote mathematical statistics and probability internationally.
+(31) 70-337-5737
isi@cbs.nl

Canadian Mathematical Society (www.math.ca)
CMS forms partnerships in business, governments, universities, and educators as well as other mathematical associations.
(613) 733-2662
office@cms.math.ca

The Council for African and Americans in the Mathematical Sciences (htt//www.math.buffalo.edu/mad/CAARMS/CAARMS-index.html)
CAARMS encourages African American and other minority group participation in mathematics.
mad_mail@yahoo.com

Clay Mathematics Institute (www.claymath.org)
CMI works to educate scientists, encourage gifted students, and recognize achievements in mathematical research.
(617) 995-2600
general@claymath.org

Consortium for Mathematics (www.comap.com)
COMAP seeks to improve mathematics education for students in elementary, high-school and college.
(800) 772-6627
info@comap.com

European Mathematical Society (www.emis.de)
EMIS works to further the development of mathematics in the countries of Europe.
+(358) 91-915-1507
ems-office@helsinki.fi

Mathematical Association of America (www.maa.org)
MAA is the largest professional society focusing on mathematics accessibility at the undergraduate level.
(800) 741-9415
maahq@maa.org

The Math Forum (www.mathforum.org)
The Forum works to improve math teaching with puzzles, math tools, online mentoring and professional development.
(800) 756-7823
contact@mathforum.org

National Association of Mathematicians (www.nam-math.org)
NAM promotes excellence in the mathematical sciences of underrepresented minorities.
(302) 857-7059
dawnalott@aol.com

National Council of Supervisors of Math (www.mathedleadership.org)
NCSM provides professional learning opportunities to support student achievement.
(303) 758-9611
office@ncsmonline.org

National Council of Teachers of Mathematics (www.nctm.org)
NCTM is the world's largest mathematics education organization, serving teachers, from elementary school through college.
(703) 620-9840
nctm@nctm.org

Society for Industrial and Applied Mathematics (www.siam.org)
SIAM promotes the development of the mathematical methods needed in a variety of areas.
(215) 382-9800
service@siam.org

Society of Actuaries (www.soa.org)
SOA strives to enhance the ability of actuaries to provide advice and solutions involving uncertain future events.
(847) 706-3500
customerservice@soa.org

TODOS: Mathematics for All! (www.todos-math.org)
TODOS works to advocate for equitable and high quality mathematics education, particularly for Hispanic/Latino students.
requests@todos-math.org

Math Books

40 Fabulous Math Mysteries Kids Can't Resist
Martin Lee, Scholastic, 2001

Brain Quest: Math 1000 Questions and Answers
Mel Jaffe and Chris Welles Feder, Workman Publishing, 2006

Go Figure! A Totally Cool Book about Numbers
Johnny Ball, DK Publishing, 2005

The Grapes of Math: Mind Stretching Math Riddles
Greg Tang, Scholastic Press, 2001

How To Solve It: A New Apect of Mathematical Model
G. Polya, Princeton University Press, 2004

Math Games and Activities from Around the World
Claudia Zaslavsky, Chicago Review Press, 1998

Math Smarts: Tips for Learning, Using, and Remembering Math
Lynette Long, Pleasant Company Publications, 2004

Math Wizardry for Kids
Margaret Kenda and Phyllis S. Williams, Barron's, 2009

Mathematical Scandals
Theoni Pappas, Wide World Publishing, 1997

One Minute Mysteries: 65 Short Mysteries You Solve with Math!
Eric and Natalie Yoder, Science, Naturally!, 2010

Stop Faking It! Math
William C. Robertson, Ph.D., NSTA Press, 2006

Stories with Holes, Volumes 1-20
Nathan Levy, NL Associates, 2005

Math Products and Websites

Online Conversion: Convert just about anything to anything else
www.OnlineConversion.com

Calculate Me: Unit Conversion
www.CalculateMe.com

Carolina Mathematics: World Class Support for Science and Math
www.carolina.com/home.do

ENASCO Math Catalog: Fun math supplies for teachers and students alike
www.enasco.com/math

ETA Cuisenaire: Educational manipulatives and supplemental materials
www.etacuisenaire.com/index.jsp

Everyday Math: A rigorous PreK-6 curriculum used across the country
www.EverydayMath.com

GIMPS: Internet Prime Number search
www.mersenne.org

Math Playground: A collection of math manipulatives for growing and learning
www.mathplayground.com

MATHematics illuminated: A 13-part course on the theories, history, and beauty of mathematics
www.learner.org/courses/mathilluminated

Math Competitions

American Regions Mathematics League Competition
(www.arml.com/index.php)
This annual competition brings students together to meet, compete against, and socialize with one another.
(310) 383-3499
ARML.Local@gmail.com

Continental Mathematics League Competition
(www.continentalmathematicsleague.com)
This competition helps students improve their reading comprehension and problem solving skills.
(631) 584-2016
cmleague@optonline.net

Homeschool Math Contests (www.homeschoolmathcontests.com/default.aspx)
Math contests for home schooled children geared to make math fun and motivate learning.
information@HomeschoolMathContests.com

International Mathematical Olympiad (www.imo-official.org)
IMO is the World Championship Mathematics Competition for high school students. Participants come from over 100 countries.
+(27) 21-650-3193
john.webb@uct.ac.za

Mathematics Competition (www.unl.edu/amc/)
AMC is dedicated to strengthening the mathematical capabilities of youth by identifying, recognizing and rewarding excellence in mathematics.
(800) 527-3690
amcinfo@maa.org

MathCounts (mathcounts.org)
MATHCOUNTS is a national enrichment, coaching and competition program that promotes middle school mathematics.
(703) 299-9006
info@mathcounts.org

The Mandelbrot Competition (www.mandelbrot.org)
This competition covers topics such as algebra, geometry, exponents, probability, number theory, and classical inequalities.
info@mandelbrot.org

Table of References

Equations

Factorial (n!)	$n! = n \times (n-1) \times (n-2) \times (n-3) \times \ldots \times 3 \times 2 \times 1$ For example: $4! = 4 \times 3 \times 2 \times 1 = 24$
Combination	The *combination* of n things taken m at a time: $n^c m = \frac{n!}{m!\,(n-m)!}$
Permutation	The *permutation* of n things taken m at a time: $n^p m = \frac{n!}{(n-m)!}$

Conversions

Units	Multiplied by	Units	Multiplied by	Units
Inches	2.54	Centimeters	0.39370	inches
Inches	25.4	Millimeters	0.03937	Inches
Inches	0.0254	Meters	39.37008	Inches
Inches	0.08333	Feet	12.0	Inches
Inches	0.02778	yards	36.0	Inches
Feet	0.33333	Yards	3.0	Feet
Feet	0.00019	Miles	5280.0	Feet
Yards	0.00057	Miles	1760.0	Yards
pound	0.45359	kilogram	2.20462	pound
ounce	0.06250	pound	16.0	ounce
ounce	0.02835	kilogram	35.27396	ounce
gram	0.00100	kilogram	1000.0	gram
ounce	28.34952	gram	0.03527	ounce
gram	0.00220	pound	453.59229	gram
pound	0.00050	ton	2000.0	pound
kilogram	0.00100	metric ton	1000.0	kilogram
pound	0.00045	metric ton	2204.62442	pound
kilogram	0.00110	ton	907.18500	kilogram
teaspoon	0.33333	tablespoon	3.00	teaspoon
cup	0.5000	pint	2.00	cup
cup	0.2500	quart	4.00	cup
cup	0.0625	gallon	16.00	cup
pint	0.5000	quart	2.00	pint
pint	0.1250	gallon	8.00	pint
quart	0.2500	gallon	4.00	quart
fluid ounce	0.125	cup	8.00	fluid ounce
tablespoon	0.5	fluid ounce	2.00	tablespoon

Formulas

Circumference of a circle	$C = 2\pi R = \pi D$ 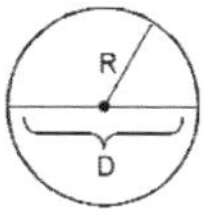
Area of a triangle	$A = \frac{1}{2} HB$ 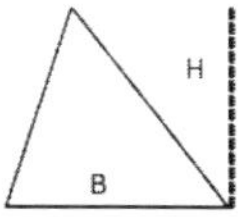
Area of a rectangle	$A = HB$ 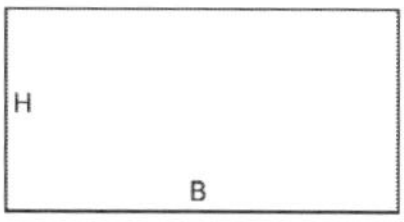
Area of a circle	$A = \pi R^2 = \frac{1}{2} RC$ 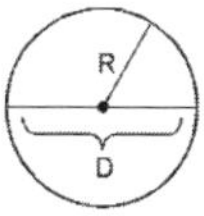
Volume of a cube	$V = L^3$ 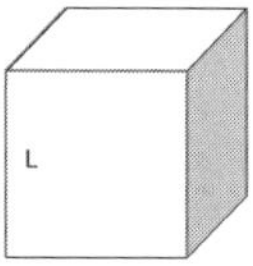
Volume of a sphere	$V = \frac{4}{3} \pi R^3$ 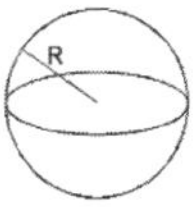
Volume of a cylinder	$V = \pi R^2 H$ 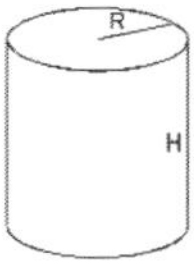
Volume of a cone	$V = \frac{1}{3} \pi R^2 H$ 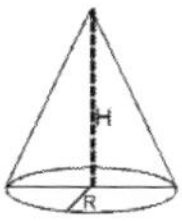

Glossary

abscissa	The x coordinate on the Cartesian plane.
acute	An angle that is less than 90 degrees.
algebra	A mathematical process used for solving equations in which letters stand for unknown or variable quantities.
algorithm	A series of steps used for solving a problem.
area	The amount of space enclosed by a two-dimensional object.
arithmetic	Basic mathematics consisting of addition, subtraction, multiplication, division and exponentiation.
average	The arithmetic mean found by adding the value of two or more items and then dividing by the total number of items.
binary	A base two numbering system.
calorie	A unit of heat equal to the amount necessary to raise the temperature of one gram of water one degree Celsius.
circumference	The perimeter of a circle.
combination	Something that is formed by joining or mixing together several things. The number of ways a group can be selected where the order of the items *does not* matter.
composite	Any whole number that is evenly divisible by one, itself and at least one other whole number.
coordinate	A number that defines position with reference to a fixed point or system of lines.

decimal	A number written in the base 10 system.
denominator	The bottom part of a fraction, as the 4 in $^1/_4$. The divisor of the numerator.
diameter	A straight line passing through the center of a circle having its ends on the circumference.
digits	One of the numerals in a number. Any of the ten numerals from 0 to 9.
ellipse	An oval with the form $ax^2 + by^2 = c$.
equator	The circle around the earth that is the same distance from both the North and South Poles.
exponent	A symbol placed to the upper-right of another, to denote the power to which the other is to be raised.
factorial	The product of whole numbers less than or equal to a specific whole number, such as $4! = 4 \times 3 \times 2 \times 1 = 24$.
finite	Limited in number.
geometry	The study of shapes.
hexadecimal	A base sixteen numbering system.
horizontal	Straight across, parallel to the horizon or a base line.
hyperbola	A conic section consisting of two identical but opposite curves, which may be defined as $ax^2 - bx^2 = c$
infinite	Unlimited; not finite; without beginning or end.
interest	A percentage that is charged on a loan or earned on an investment.
irrational	A number not capable of being expressed as a ratio of two whole numbers.

latitude The angular distance between the equator and a point north or south on the earth's surface.

logarithm A number that represents the power to which a certain number must be raised to equal some other given number.

longitude The angular distance on the earth's surface east or west of the Prime Meridian at Greenwich, England.

mathematics The study of numbers.

numerator The top part of a fraction, as the 3 in $^3/_4$. It is the number that will be divided by the denominator.

obtuse An angle greater than 90 degrees and less than 180 degrees.

ordinate The y coordinate on the Cartesian plane.

parabola A curve that is formed by the intersection of a right, circular cone and a plane that is parallel to a straight line up the side of the cone, represented generally as $y = ax^2 + bx + c$.

parallel Planes or lines that are the same distance from each other at every corresponding point.

permutation The number of ways a group can be selected where the order of the items *does* matter.

perpendicular Forming a right angle with an intersecting line or plane.

pi (π) A mathematical constant equaling the ratio of the circumference of a circle to its diameter, estimated as 3.14159 or $^{22}/_7$.

polygon A two-dimensional figure with three or more sides consisting of straight lines.

prime Any whole number that is divisible only by one and itself.

principal The deposit part of an investment, as opposed to the earnings generated by it.

probability A number expressing the degree of likelihood of an occurrence, where 0 represents impossibility and 1 expresses certainty.

proof A logical way to verify the correctness of a solution.

quadrilateral Any polygon consisting of four sides.

rational A number able to be expressed in the form $^a/_b$ where a and b are whole numbers.

square root A divisor of a quantity that when multiplied by itself gives the quantity. For example, the square roots of 25 are 5 and -5 because 5 x 5 = 25 and (-5) x (-5) = 25.

statistics The study of numerical information.

symmetry An event in which parts on opposite sides of a plane, line, or point display the same form; a balance of size, shape and arrangement.

tessellation The fitting of shapes together to form a design or picture.

vertex The point of intersection of the two sides of an angle, or of three or more planes of a three-dimensional object.

vertical Straight up and down.

volume The amount of space enclosed by a three-dimensional object.

Index by Subject Area

About the Authors

Marc Zev is an engineer who has published in the fields of Structural Mechanics and Information Technology. He is founder and president of the Foundation for Innovative Learning, a non-profit dedicated to enhancing the problem-solving abilities of children and adults. He also owns Pensive Products, which creates educational tools, such as Math Flaps, a manipulative specifically designed to teach division. He lives in Chatsworth, California with his wife, two sons, four finches and dog. He can be reached at Marc@ScienceNaturally.com.

Kevin B. Segal has a Bachelor's in Pure Mathematics and a Master's in Applied Mathematics, both from California State University, Fullerton. He also completed four years of post-graduate studies in Applied Mathematics at UCLA. An Associate of the Society of Actuaries, he now works as a "charismatic number cruncher." He lives in Chatsworth, California with his wife, daughter, and son. He can be reached at Kevin@ScienceNaturally.com.

Nathan Levy is a prolific writer. Some of his books include *Stories with Holes, Whose Clues* and *101 Things Everyone Should Know About Science.* A gifted educator, Nathan worked directly with children, teachers and parents in his 35 years as a teacher and principal. He has mentored more than 30 principals and superintendents and trained thousands of teachers in strategies that encourage the love of learning. A resident of Hightstown, NJ, he leads workshops for educators and parents. He can be reached at Nathan@ScienceNaturally.com.

About Science, Naturally!

Science, Naturally! is committed to increasing science and math literacy by exploring and demystifying educational topics in fun and entertaining ways. Our mission is to produce products—for children and adults alike—filled with interesting facts, important insights and key connections. Our products are perfect for kids, parents, educators and anyone interested in gaining a better understanding of how science and math affect everyday life.

Our materials are designed to engage readers by using both fiction and nonfiction strategies to teach potentially intimidating topics. Some of the country's premier science organizations designate our materials among the best available and highly recommend them as supplemental resources for science teachers. In fact, **all** of our titles have been awarded the coveted "NSTA Recommends" designation.

You can listen to audio versions of our books, enjoy author interviews and explore our multimedia resources (including iPhone applications) at www.SoundbiteScience.com, your source for all our audio, electronic and mp3 selections.

For more information about our publications, to request a catalog, to be added to our mailing list, or to learn more about becoming a *Science, Naturally!* author, give us a call or visit us online.

Science, Naturally! books are distributed by National Book Network in the U.S. and abroad and by Mariposa Press in France.

Science, Naturally!®
725 8th Street, SE
Washington, DC 20003
202-465-4798
Toll-free: 1-866-SCI-9876
(1-866-724-9876)
Fax: 202-558-2132
Info@ScienceNaturally.com
www.ScienceNaturally.com

Make your mark in education—
Submit a Question

We are always looking for engaging questions for our "101 Things Everyone Should Know" series. Submit a question for our "101 Things Everyone Should Know" books. If you have a great math or science question, we want to know it! If we use it, we'll send you a free copy of the book in which it appears.

Email your question to: 101Things@ScienceNaturally.com

Or send it to us at;

101 Things Submission
Science, Naturally!
725 8th Street SE
Washington, DC 20003

Test Booklet Information

Use *101 Things Everyone Should Know About Math* with a group of students!

Science, Naturally! has created a student test booklet, available for classroom, home-school, after-school, or math club use.

The booklet (ISBN: 978-0-9678020-2-2) includes all 106 questions from this book. Use as a single write-in test booklet or have students write the answers on a separate sheet.

Order today! Contact us at Info@ScienceNaturally.com.

QUANTITY	PRICE
1-9	$2.95 each
10+	$1.77 each
50+	$1.47 each
100+	$1.33 each
250+	$1.18 each
500+	$1.03 each
1000+	$ .89 each

If you loved this book, don't miss...

101 Things Everyone Should Know About Science

By Dia L. Michels and Nathan Levy

"Succinct, cleverly written...should be on everyone's bookshelf!"

—Katrina L. Kelner, Ph.D. *Science* Magazine

"Readers will devour the book and be left eager for the 102nd thing to know!" —Margaret Kenda, *Science Wizardry for Kids*

"Their book challenges our understanding, intrigues us and leads us on a voyage of discovery!"

—April Holladay, author, *WonderQuest.com*

Why do you see lightning before you hear thunder? What keeps the planets orbiting around the Sun? Why do we put salt on roads when they are icy? What metal is a liquid at room temperature? And the burning question: Why do so many scientists wear white lab coats?

Science affects everything—yet so many of us wish we understood it better. Using an engaging question-and-answer format, key concepts in biology, chemistry, physics, earth science and general science are explored and demystified. Endorsed by science organizations and educators, this easy-to-tackle book is a powerful tool to assess and increase science literacy. Perfect for kids, parents, educators and anyone interested in gaining a better understanding of how science impacts everyday life.

Ages 8-12
ISBN 978-0-9678020-5-3
Paperback $9.95

One Minute Mysteries: 65 Short Mysteries You Solve With Science!

By Eric Yoder and Natalie Yoder

These short mysteries, each just one minute long, have a fun and intersting twist—you have to tap into your knowledge of science to solve them! Enjoy 65 brain twisters that challenge your knowledge of science in everyday life.

"Turns kids into scientists...stimulating and great fun for the whole family!" —Katrina L. Kelner, Ph.D., Science Magazine

"Parents and kids alike will be challenged... A great way to grow a young scientist—or improve an old one!"
—Julie Edmonds, Carnegie Academy for Science Education

As heard on National Public Radio

Audio renditions of selected mysteries can be heard at www.SoundbiteScience.com and www.REALscience.us.

Ages 8-12
ISBN: 978-0-9678020-1-5
Paperback: $9.95

One Minute Mysteries: 65 Short Mysteries You Solve With Math!

By Eric Yoder and Natalie Yoder

The second book in our wildly successful "One Minute Mysteries" series, *One Minute Mysteries: 65 Short Mysteries You Solve With Math!* keeps you entertained and eager to learn more! These short mysteries, each just one minute long, have a fun and interesting twist—you have to tap into your mathematical wisdom to solve them! Solve 65 math brain twisters that challenge your knowledge of math in everyday life!

As much fun as the first book in the series, *One Minute Mysteries: 65 Short Mysteries You Solve With Science!*, this educational book is easy to use at home, in school or even in the car. Great for kids, grown-ups, educators and anyone who loves good mysteries, good math problems or both!

"...real-life situations with solutions that would make Encyclopedia Brown jealous." —Clay Kaufman, Co-Director, Siena School

"...skillfully meshes humor and excitement with challenging problems."
—Rachel Connelly, Ph.D., Bowdoin College

"...fabulous resource for kids, parents and teachers looking for a way to link mathematics to everyday life."
—Carole Basile, Ed.D., University of Colorado, Denver

Ages 10-14
ISBN: 978-0-9678020-0-8
Paperback $9.95

If My Mom Were a Platypus: Mammal Babies and Their Mothers

By Dia L. Michels • Illustrated by Andrew Barthelmes

"As engaging visually as it is verbally!"

—Dr. Ines Cifuentes, Carnegie Academy for Science Education

"The animal facts . . . are completely engrossing. Most readers are sure to be surprised by something they learn about these seemingly familiar animals."

—Carolyn Baile, *ForeWord* magazine

Middle grade students learn how 14 mammals are born, eat, sleep, learn and mature. The fascinating facts depict how mammal infants begin life dependent on their mothers and grow to be self-sufficient adults. This book highlights the topics of birth, growth, knowledge and eating for 13 different animals. All stories are told from the baby's point of view. The 14th and final species is a human infant, with amazing similarities to the other stories. With stunning full color and black-and-white illustrations and concise information, this book helps children develop a keen sense of what makes mammals special.

Ages 8-12, 64 pages. Curriculum-based Activity Guide with dozens of fun, hands-on projects available free of charge at www.ScienceNaturally.com

ISBN: 978-1-930775-44-2	Hardback book	$16.95
ISBN: 978-1-930775-44-2	Hardback + 15" plush platypus	$29.95
ISBN: 978-1-930775-19-0	Paperback book	$ 9.95
ISBN: 978-1-930775-30-5	Paperback + 15" plush platypus	$22.95